THE ULTIMATE GUIDE TO
CAMPCRAFT AND ADVANCED DEEP
WOODS SKILLS...

From learning to make a shelter in the snow
to building a one-match fire in any climate or
weather,

The Master Backwoodsman

is filled with hundreds of secrets of successful
outdoor living, camping, and hiking.

Bradford Angier combines the best of all he
has learned in a lifetime, producing a wealth of
information. With this book you can learn how
to utilize the environment without spoiling it,
how to travel peaceably in the woods, and how
to enjoy camp life in the wilds for days, weeks,
and even months.

THE MASTER BACKWOODSMAN

Bradford Angier

FAWCETT COLUMBINE • NEW YORK

ISBN 0-449-90126-2

This edition published by arrangement with Stackpole Books
Photos by Russ Mohney and Bradford Angier
Drawings by Vera Angier and Roberta Fink

Manufactured in the United States of America

First Fawcett Columbine Edition: October 1979
First Ballantine Books Edition: June 1984

10   9   8   7   6   5   4   3   2   1

To James F. M. Day
—for fifty years a newspaperman and for the
last thirty years the managing editor of
The Californian, one of the world's great newspapers—
an accomplished outdoorsman who has hunted and fished
throughout the world, an honorable gentleman, a licensed
navigator, a distinguished companion, and a superb friend,
this book is humbly dedicated

Contents

CHAPTER 1

The Lure of the Backwoods

Civilization these days seems to be closing in more and more stiflingly all about us. Yet on this continent there remains real wilderness where you can still make your own way, cut firewood and browse with no harm to anyone, and answer the instinctive call of the open places while eyes will never be keener or stride more lusty. This is good, for essentially we all need the tonic of our remaining backwoods.

The trail's call is instinctive, having nothing to do with our common sense. We realize we are perhaps fools for answering it, and yet we go. The comforts of worldly conveniences, to relegate the matter to its basic level, are not to be disregarded lightly: the burden-lightening ease of having our physical labor performed for us, the agreeableness of cultivated minds, of theaters and television, of books, of keeping abreast of world developments. These we renounce. In exchange, we undertake an existence in which there is considerable hard toil—work so admittedly long and exhausting that few men paid to labor would consider it for a second.

We go back to the pioneer demands of eating simply, of enduring much, of sleeping out in storms and wind. We deliberately put ourselves where such discomforts as wet, cold and heat, hunger, thirst, danger, and monotony become a part of our lives. On numerous occasions in the self-reliance of a wilderness existence even the stoutest hearted will admit to himself privately—very privately if he is really stouthearted, so

that his companions will not falter—that if destiny allows him to get through, he will never get in such a position again.

Such occasions arise when lengthy continuances fray the spirit. We have borne a pack until every muscle is strained taut; the woods are breathless, the mosquitoes buzz about us unceasingly in spite of the repellent with which we have doused ourselves. We beat all day windward in a lone canoe toward what would normally be but a several hours' paddle: the gusts are relentless and the wind-hurled water cold; there are looming rocks and no time to eat; chill gray evening draws perilously near, and there are inches of water about our feet.

We have strived through clotting snow until every time we advance our snowshoes we have the sensation of an imp stabbing his little pitchfork into our thighs; it has darkened; the colored alcohol in the thermometer is an inch below zero, and with numbed fingers we must make an adequate camp which is only a forerunner of many more such camps to follow. For days it has driven down rain, so that we, pressing through the sodden brush, are soaked and comfortless and sweaty, and the undergrowth has lacerated our shriveling hide.

We have stealthily tracked a bull moose on the look for a lady love for two days, only dismayingly to realize he has looped back into the wind prior to coiling up for a rest, then crashed away in a black blur from an unsuspected patch of small spruce, keeping it between him and us so that we have no chance for a shot. Or we are just plain exhausted, not from a single day's tiredness but from the gradual wearing down of a long ride.

Then in our private hearts we echo these reactions: "We are idiots. This is not pleasure. There is no genuine call for us to do this. If we ever struggle out of here, we will stay home where common sense reigns!"

After awhile we do get out and are thankful. But in the next few months we will have proved to ourselves the following

truth—the most all-encompassing axiom the backwoods have to teach. It won't matter how difficult a time we have been subjected to, how little fun has been interwoven with it, for in a few months our overall reaction to that journey will be good. We will think back on the difficult times and triumph over the pictures of them with a certain joy of remembrance.

I recall one trip I took in the early fall, hunting and fishing along the wild Half Moon of New Brunswick's Southwest Miramichi River. It rained without ceasing for a week. We were wet to the hide all the time, ate standing up in the roaring campfire that evaporated some of the downpour, and slept soaked. So frosty was it in the mornings that the tarps over our sleeping bags were stiff with ice and snapped when we hauled out. But even in that torment we got our limits of fish and game. Despite that, I can appraise the ordeal as about the most ill-conceived I ever got into. Yet as a general impres-

sion, that Southwest Miramichi canoe trip comes back to me as a most enjoyable one.

Once we have been back home a bit the call of the trail starts to become audible. Initially it is extremely docile. But trifle by trifle a restlessness permeates us. At first we don't appreciate precisely what is the difficulty. We are concerned only that our everyday life has lost its savor, that we are performing tasks more or less automatically, that we are a modicum more touchy than our naturally intractable temperaments.

And slowly it comes over us precisely what is the trouble. Then we mutter to ourselves:

"Fellow, you've learned. You are no cheechako. You realize precisely how hard you will have to labor, and how many difficulties you are going to encounter, how famished, chilly, damp, weary, and generally worn out you are going to be. You've been in the bush often enough before, so it's especially vivid to you. You're getting into this thing with your eyes wide open. You know what you're going to be in for. You're mighty well set right here, and you'd be an idiot to go."

"Right you are," you agree with yourself. "You're plumb right about it all. I wonder where we can pick up another cayuse."

CHAPTER 2

Campfire: No. 1 Backwoods Necessity

The campfire, cheery and companionable, is the backwoodsman's most fundamental necessity. The average tenderfoot, when he becomes turned around in the woods, immediately begins fearing starvation, death from thirst, and peril from dangerous animals. There is almost never any reason for the first, seldom any for the second, and none on this continent for the third aside from rabidity, and the occasional polar bear or grizzly. Exposure, on the other hand, can kill you in a few minutes.

With a campfire, though, we can warm and dry ourselves, relish a night in comfort and safety, cook the meals which we'll consider later to be of nearly limitless scope and, if necessary, signal for help. None of us, therefore, should travel through or over the wild places anywhere at any time without the knowledge and means of building an emergency fire in the course of daily living.

When you are alone or with a small party, the making of campfires should be approached with due thought and preparation, not blithely, casually, and desultorily—the way one sees too many nincompoops tackling the problem. For instance, what is the most common reason for accidental death in the Far North? It is not cold, but fire. One doesn't even have to look that far afield. Consider the outdoor conflagrations of civilization, some of them started by natural causes, such as lightning, or by some reasonably unavoidable accident. But far too many life-and-property-destroying blazes are begun by fools. Never take any chances.

The way to be ready for that possible crisis in the backwoods, when a successful campfire may make the difference between comfort and misery or even life and death, is to go about lighting every fire as if you have only one match. In New Brunswick, a required-by-law guide who got lost when we were hunting apart in unfamiliar country nearly froze to death the stormy night he was out, not because he did not have several matches and an unlimited quantity of good tinder and fuel, but because he was in the habit of having a large quantity of paper and matches at hand when it became time to start the campfire. He had come to regard fire-making as a triviality.

The Boy Scout requirement for learning to start a campfire with no more than two matches and only natural fuel is a sound one, and was what probably made me serious about being able to start a blaze in every situation, no matter what

the conditions. I don't think this can be overemphasized even today.

Such certain and sure fire-making often takes a lot more time than many individuals are inclined to give it, but this is one aspect of good woodsmanship that should never be hurried. What keeps the average person from developing this skill is that campfires are usually easily handled and that, if one falls short of matches, the other fellow generally has plenty.

The hardest time I ever had in starting and retaining a campfire was after a Northeast week of drizzly, windy, frosty weather, when rain was falling and constantly adding to the coating of ice that seemed to sheathe every twig. Wet and miserable, I had been out a week in unfamiliar country on my own, and I had only two matches left in my waterproof match case. What to do? I was in my teens and had a lot to learn, as I still do.

Well, at least I was in softwood country where spruce, interspersed with occasional birch, were so plentiful that today I wouldn't give the matter a second thought. Incidentally, I had belted to my waist the best six-inch sheath knife with attached sharpening stone that I could afford, even though at that time one of these was regarded by all too many as the sign of a tenderfoot.

There wasn't a dry foot of ground anywhere on which it was reasonable to make a fire, so the first thing I did was to strip large sheets of birch bark from some living trees—this being utter wilderness—to floor a space in front of a thickly needled young fir into which I had stripped a niche in which to sit. I put a sheet of bark to sit on in here, too, where at least it wouldn't get any wetter.

I then cut a third sheet of bark from another birch, which incidentally wouldn't kill the tree, and divided this into thin, dry, paperlike scraps which, filled with oil as they were, could be depended on to burst into flame, giving off a heavy, sweet, black smoke when—facing the wind so that the fire would eat down the stick—I applied one of my hand-and-body-shielded matches to it. I stored these bits of bark beneath the largest curling sheet.

Source of Kindling
Dry, dead, resinous twigs and branches on the lower trunks of all
evergreens make good kindling.

On the bottoms of all thick, small evergreens there are masses of tiny dead twigs that are full of resin. These could be counted on to ignite from the tiny scraps of birch bark. In turn, they would start burning the larger limbs of well-protected and fairly dry spruce that I collected and turned into what I knew as fuzzsticks: one-foot lengths of straight-grained wood on which I cut curl after dry curl, detaching as few as possible and saving these for additional tinder.

But softwood won't hold a fire, so I found a standing dead poplar, broke several heavy limbs from it by my weight, reduced these by levering them between two rocks, scraped the ice from them, and then made them into kindling with my boots. Some old, upright, softwood stubs of trunks were about, remains of an ancient fire. They were pretty well rotted, but I kicked enough of them apart to get a number of tough, resin-rich knots.

I made and covered with birch bark a square-foot space in front of the niche where I intended to retreat. Then on the heavy birch bark which, incidentally, is flammable even though wet, I carefully piled my wisps of birch bark. I added in turn the closely amassed twigs, and, in a well-ventilated wigwam, the fuzzsticks, the poplar kindling, and finally a few of the resinous knots. This, I figured, would make a fire hot enough to dry out and burn the large, standing, dead poplar limbs that I heaped loosely over everything.

Then I applied one of my two precious matches to the shielded little nest of birch wisps. It caught. It worked.

I broiled my tenderloin venison kabobs on a sharpened green willow while comfortable on my water-impervious seat within the cavity whose back was toward the wind. I suspended my large can of tea water by its wire bail from another green willow limb, pressed into the ground at one end and

Fuzzsticks

B'iling the Kettle

held at the proper height at the other end by a forked green stick. Warm, sated, and refreshed, I continued with my packboard load of deer meat to my river camp and canoe, well ahead of the advancing winter.

DAY-BY-DAY CAMPFIRE LIGHTING

The most satisfactory everyday method of lighting campfires is with the common, strike-anywhere, wooden, so-called "kitchen" match. Besides carrying for daily use one to a pocket (because of the then-lessened risk of their accidentally rubbing together and lighting), you'll always want to have on your person in the wilderness a sufficient nucleus of matches for emergency use. This is in addition to carrying in the outfit a supply, sufficient for even an over-extended trip, in a large, waterproof, unbreakable plastic container. If there is any doubt that the container is impervious to moisture, water-proof it with tape or melted paraffin. An old technique still good today is to waterproof matches loosely packed in a large box by carefully, slowly, and completely filling the box with melted wax. Individual matches, their sticks then candlelike and more flammable, can be broken one by one from the block.

How and where to carry the daily nucleus? Well, a reasonably alert individual is all the time learning. I've long borne two filled, waterproof cases on my person while in the backwoods on the reasonable principle of hoping for the best but preparing for the worst. One of these has always been what is still the soundest container I have ever seen on the market: a handy, small, metallic, easily unscrewed (even with numbed and wet fingers) Marble match case with a ring on top for pinning to the clothing. These are obtainable at many of the better sporting goods stores and from the Marble Arms Corporation, Gladstone, Michigan 49837.

At a sportsman's show in Boston years ago a company gave me a black bakelite container that held more matches and was certainly convenient. I started using that for my everyday supply until one morning, wading for arctic grayling and rainbow trout along Maurice Creek in northeast British Columbia, I fell on a slimy stone, and there was the bakelite case shattered and its contents saturated. From that day on I have always carried my two unbreakable Marble cases.

Another thing I learned from experience, from having that bakelite case full of matches explode from the top in my hand—harmlessly, fortunately, and on the other side of the continent this time—is that the match tops may be rubbed

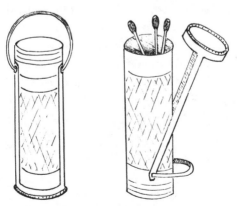

Marble Match Case
Left: **Closed.** *Right:* **Open.**

together in the closing of the receptacle. The solution was to store half of the matches upside down. You can pack more this way, too.

The small boxes of safety matches and the packs of paper matches, freely available all over the world for advertising purposes, are too fragile and shortlived for the wilderness. If you care to carry a few of these for random use, particularly if you are a smoker, at least enclose each packet in something like foil to protect it from the dampness of precipitation, humidity, and perspiration.

THE METAL MATCH

The only recent invention of personal significance to the outdoorsman, outside of such things as fabrics and some of the new zippers, is the Metal Match. This is now manufactured and sold by Palco Products, Box 88, Slatersville, Rhode Island 02876. If your sporting goods store does not yet stock it, inquiries regarding availability of this unique and efficient product should be directed to the maker. One belongs in every outdoorsman's outfit.

The Metal Match is made of eleven rare earth metals extruded from inert gas under extremely high pressures. The result is a short, grayish stick that is waterproof, fireproof, non-toxic, and reasonably durable (except after prolonged exposure to humidity) and that, depending on its size, will ignite between 1000 and 3000 fires.

One is quickly and simply used. Just shave a few tiny bits from the Match with the back of a knife or any hard, keen substance, such as a rock. These fragments are grouped in a small space—amid wisps of birch bark or other tinder if you're starting a campfire—and lit with a spark produced from the Metal Match with a rapid downward motion of the same knife back, rock, or such. The spark carries heat of 2800°F, but because of the brief time that sparks are in existence, the Metal Match is safe in even inexperienced hands. It can also be used to light camp stoves and such. The Metal Match will really round out an outdoor outfit, from the simplest to the most elaborate.

CAMPFIRES IN GENERAL

Incidentally, there is no need to disfigure the beautiful birch, even in the deepest forest, to get enough tinder for your day-by-day fires. Just a handful of the flutters of bark, which can be pulled harmlessly from any such tree, will do the job with less trouble.

The campfire, your most cheerful companion in the bush, is started with a spark or flame to which is added tinder, kindling, and then the hottest and longest lasting fuel you can come by. You should always make certain that you have matches or, if you are traveling especially lightly and compactly, at least a Metal Match. Lacking either, usually by inadequate planning or accident, you may produce a spark by one of several simple methods or by the more laborious and time-consuming methods of rubbing wood against wood, as detailed in such survival manuals as my *Living Off the Country* and *Survival with Style*.

With sufficient sunlight, a magnifier (such as a pocket lens, a camera or binocular lens, or even distorted glass from a bottle) will do the job quickly and efficiently. In addition, a full-page magnifier, which is an inexpensive, thin, unbreakable, light, flat, and easily packed sheet of magnifying plastic, is effective. A nine-by-twelve magnifier was sent to me for successful below-zero experimentation by a reader, Glenn B. Dudley of San Francisco. Mr. Dudley wrote that he got mine for less than a dollar from Sunset House, 1288 Culver Boulevard, Los Angeles, California 90066. Similar devices are cheaply available from other mail-order houses.

If you have spare cartridges or shells, the carefully extracted powder from one of these can be safely lighted with tinder by rubbing it between two smooth, dry stones. Daniel Boone's flint and steel works as well as it did during pioneer days, or you may strike the back of your ax, hatchet, or knife experimentally against some other hard stone. Even two rocks, such as fool's gold, may spark when struck together.

Tinder is the next requirement and becomes more critical when you are without matches. Anything dry and highly flammable will do: cotton or woolen lint from your clothing, absorbent cotton or gauze from your first aid kit, down from plants, pulverized dead grass or conifer needles, down, bone-dry nests, insect-rendered dust found behind the bark of some dead trees, the fluffy brown coverings of the apiang palm, the dry substances seen at the base of coconut leaves, dry bat droppings, and the like.

Kindling depends upon where you are. As a rule, it should come from dead wood, perhaps driftwood, which has not been in recent contact with the ground. Exceptions occur during prolonged dry spells and in the case of woods, like the living birch and ash, which burn much better when green. Dry softwoods, with their highly flammable resins, are in general better for kindling than are hardwoods. Making three or four fuzzsticks, previously described, as the nucleus of the blaze provides a surer fire. Fuzzsticks are surpassed mainly by the chips and shavings produced when you're making a log cabin with seasoned logs such as spruce, lodgepole pine, and the like. The so-called hardwoods in general produce longer lasting, hotter, less sparking, and therefore safer campfires.

Rather than trying to remember the sequence of heat-producing woods, led in North America by hickory, experiment with what is at hand, the rule being that heaviness and warmth go together. Besides, you'll have to make out with what you have. In the desert this may be dry animal dung, reminiscent of the frontiersman's buffalo chips, and any twigs, stems, roots, and brush that may be at hand. In the Far North it may be blubber, the tiny heatherlike evergreen that will readily burn even when wet and green, mosses, lichens, willow and other brush, and certainly driftwood.

SAFETY

Anyplace where fire can disastrously spread, make absolutely sure of the safety of the surrounding countryside as well

as of your outfit. Dig or heel down preferably to mineral soil for an adequate space all around before you begin. Be extremely wary of sparks, especially in wind.

When you are done with the campfire, make sure every last bit is extinguished, particularly the often disregarded roots which can smolder all winter under deep snow, only to burst into a devastating forest fire in the warmness of spring. If you can, douse everything with water before you leave and mix the ashes in your hand until absolutely no warmth remains in them. Carefully check everything nearby to make certain that no sparks have left a continuing danger.

FIREPLACES

Fireplaces are not a part of the backwoodsman's day-by-day technique, for they are not only unnecessarily time-consuming but also potentially dangerous in two respects. The rocks often selected by the novice or occasional woods frequenter are apt to be the smoothly rounded stones from a stream bed, and some of these may contain moisture that can and does cause dangerous explosions when heated. Also, fire is apt to creep and stay beneath and between the rocks of such a fireplace.

The most a sourdough usually does is to kindle his blaze behind a nonflammable bank, the earthy back of a huge fallen tree, perhaps a pile of rocks, or, frequently for the long night fire beside which he bivouacs, before a wall of green or dead logs held by outwardly slanting rocks so that besides being a reflector they can feed the fire during the night hours. These methods have a purpose other than heat reflection. Smoke, attracted by large objects such as human beings, actually does follow you as you seek to escape it by changing your position, and such a reflector helps control the draft.

All that the usual outdoorsman does to control his cooking fire is to build it between two preferably green logs, not birch or ash, which have been laid in a long, tight "V" with the wider opening toward the wind. These logs should be close enough together that they can be spanned by the frypan and

Cooking Fire

by any cooking pots that do not have bails on which they can be suspended. (Such suspension can be accomplished by forked sticks of the desired lengths, each with a handle-holding notch at the lower end, that are hung from a long green pole held over the blaze by forked green sticks driven into the ground at either end of the heat.)

Incidentally, do not look for the photogenic forked stick seen in many illustrations, mainly because one would be difficult to pound in. Instead, settle for a stout green pole with a

branch stub at the desired height. The same thing is true
when you are holding up a single nonflammable pole whose
lower extremity is held in place by a heavy object or by being
sharpened and pressed into the soil—all that the backwoodsman does when b'iling the tea kettle at midday, almost a
ritual in the North Woods. A large fruit juice can, its top
smoothly removed and a wire bail strung between two holes
punched on opposites sides just below the rim, serves for this
ceremony. I always carry a foil-wrapped wad of black tea,
desired proportions being arrived at through practice. I also
like bite-size kabobs roasted over the fire on a green wand, or
sandwiches toasted on a forked green stick for the noonday
pickup. The rest, refreshment, and stimulation of such a practice helps along the robust continuation of the day's activities.

Above timberline and in the desert, when fuel is sparse and
the wind perhaps high, the best fireplace is made by heeling

or otherwise making a furrow parallel to the air currents and narrow enough to be spanned by the cooking utensils, and then building the fire in that.

Snow and ice seldom present more problems than they solve by the availability of water obtained by melting. In the forest, getting fuel is hardly ever difficult, although in the barrens you may have to dig or otherwise provide for it, as with the mountaineer's primus stove. But much of the Far North, where the preponderance of the remaining wilderness lies today, is semi-arid and the snowfall scant. You can build your temporary fire atop the snow, possible on a flooring of green branches, or in less severe conditions scoop your way to solid ground, being careful in either event to do this in the open or where snow tumbling from laden trees will not extinguish your possibly hard-won efforts.

NIGHT FIRE

If you are camping in the open and desire a fire for warmth as well as for companionship, the trick is to build one as long as your body and sleep between the fire and some reflector such as a large rock. At the same time, the fire itself should be reflected by some such arrangement as a slanting wall of green logs, held up by poles or stakes. This is a technique that determines at a glance the difference between a cheechako and a sourdough. No matter how large you make your fire, seldom will it last the night. The best procedure is to gather a large pile of firewood by your head so that you must only lean up on one elbow to lay fresh fuel into place.

Unless you were utterly exhausted when you retired, the encroaching cold will awaken you for this chore. In the morning, if you have planned well, a glowing bed of coals will remain for cooking your breakfast.

Far from being hardships, these occasional rousings in the peaceful intensity of darkness, serene and mysterious as from the sources of life, are memorable respites. Perhaps the timber wolves, no danger to any man except on the very, very rare occasions when one is rabid, are howling with all the

Reflecting a Fire

In extreme cold, sit between fire and reflecting surface.

beautiful, sweet intensity denied those who elect to remain behind in the cities. A pair of owls may enliven the peacefulness with their hoo-hoo-hooing. Sparks soar straight up toward Orion's belted brightness, and perhaps you mark the position of Polaris so that in the daylight you can check your compass's local declination. Then almost instantly you are back asleep.

CHAPTER 3

Shelter: No. 2 Requirement

Holding to the truth that exposure is the backwoods' surest and swiftest killer, we must concede that shelter is second only to fire in importance. This shelter need not be at all elaborate, depending of course on the adequacy of your clothing and your sleeping provisions.

"A comfortable home was once made here almost entirely of such materials as Nature furnished," Henry David Thoreau noted more than a century ago. "Consider how slight a shelter is absolutely necessary."

Although this is still very true, invading civilization has opened so many tracts of what we once considered to be wilderness that only a portion is left of what the mountain men, trappers, early prospectors, and timber cruisers once considered to be virgin territory. Yet millions of unspoiled acres remain, in prime pockets here and there and in immense stretches along the roof of the continent where, as the saying goes, the hand of man has seldom set foot.

Here we can still go and build lean-tos, make browse beds, and sit at night by a lone campfire with the yips of coyotes our only companions. This is the country for the canoeist, the backpacker, the individual who's handy with a diamond hitch, and the pilot of a small plane with pontoons.

We can no longer fell trees, feed night fires, or blaze a trail in much of the former wilderness that is now the domain of the paid guide, the snowmobile, the outboard motor, and the four-wheel-drive vehicle. But the modern adventurer who wants to escape the concrete chasms and the asphalt jungles and to depend entirely on his own God-given abilities can— with determination and a bit of hard work at first, before he settles into the ease of the true woodsman who has already tasted the joys of roughing it and is now smoothing the way for himself well back of beyond—find the real backwoods that we are considering in this volume. Thereafter, what may have seemed hardships on the fringes of the settled places will, beyond the domain of the snowmobile and the trail bike, be to him merely a moderate amount of vacationing exercise.

The niche in a Christmas tree, described in the last chapter, so simple to contrive that I often make one in perhaps five minutes for nestling in while boiling the kettle at noon on a stormy day, is perfectly adequate for an overnight shelter if you sit on a warm browse bed on the side opposite the wind with your back to the trunk, strip or cut off no more than enough additional boughs to contain yourself snugly, and build a small campfire in front, with sufficient dead, dry wood within easy reaching distance to keep it burning all night.

Security from wind and cold can be intensified, in other words, if you intersperse the living boughs with others shoved in from other trees. First, of course, shake such an evergreen free of snow if necessary. To keep out further moisture in stormy weather, roof the opening with something such as birch bark. For years I have carried an eight-by-ten-foot sheet of plastic that is so thin it can handily be folded into a breast pocket of my shirt and is always available to solve any such roofing problems.

THE INDIAN CAMP

"The simplest and most primitive of all camps is the 'Indian Camp,'" Colonel Townsend Whelen's old friend Nessmuk— George W. Sears—wrote nearly a century ago. "It is easily and quickly made, is warm and comfortable, and stands a pretty heavy rain when properly put up. This is how it is made.

"Let us say you are out and have slightly missed your way. The coming gloom warns you that night is shutting down. You are no tenderfoot. You know that a place of rest is essential to health and comfort through the long, cold November night. You dive down the first little hollow until you strike a rill of water, for water is a prime necessity. As you draw your hatchet you take in the whole situation at a glance.

"The little stream is gurgling in a half choked frozen way. There is a huge soddened hemlock lying across it. One clip of the hatchet showed that it will peel. There is plenty of small timber standing about ... long, slim poles, with a tuft of foliage on top. Five minutes suffices to drop one of these, cut a twelve-foot pole from it, sharpen the pole at each end, jam one end into the ground and the other into the rough bark of a scraggly hemlock, and there is your ridge-pole.

"Now go—with your hatchet—for the bushiest and most promising young hemlocks within reach. Drop them and draw them to camp rapidly. Next, you need a fire. There are fifty hard, resinous limbs sticking up from the prone hemlock; lop off a few of these and split the largest into match timber; reduce the splinters to shavings, scrape the wet leaves from your prospective fire-place, and strike a match on the balloon part of your trousers. If you are a woodsman, you will strike but one.

"Feed the fire slowly at first; it will gain fast. When you have a blaze ten feet high, look at your watch. It is 6 p.m. You don't want to turn in before 10 o'clock, and you have four hours to kill before bed-time. Now, tackle the old hemlock; take off every dry limb, and then peel the bark and bring it to camp. You will find this takes an hour or more.

"Next, strip every limb from your young hemlocks; and shingle them onto your ridge-pole. This will make a sort of bear den, very well calculated to give you a comfortable night's rest. The bright fire will soon dry the ground that is to be your bed, and you will have plenty of time to drop another small hemlock and make a bed of browse a foot high. You do it.

"Then you make your pillow. . . . It is half a yard of muslin, sewed up as a bag, and filled with moss or hemlock browse. You can empty it and put it in your pocket, where it takes up about as much room as a handkerchief. You will have other little muslin bags—an' you be wise. One holds a couple of ounces of good tea; another, sugar; another is kept to put your loose duffle in: money, match safe, pocketknife. You have a pat of butter and a bit of pork, with a liberal slice of brown bread, and before turning in, you make a cup of tea, broil a slice of pork, and indulge in a lunch.

"Ten o'clock comes. The time has not passed tediously. You are warm, dry, and well-fed. Your old friends, the owls, come near the fire light and salute you with their strange wild notes; a distant fox sets up for himself with his odd, barking cry, and you turn in. Not ready to sleep just yet.

"But you drop off; and it is two bells in the morning watch when you waken with a sense of chill and darkness. The fire has burned low, and snow is falling. The owls have left, and a deep silence broods over the cold, still forest. You rouse the

fire, and, as the bright light shines in the furthest recesses of
your forest den, get out the little pipe, and reduce a bit of navy
plug to its lowest denomination. The smoke curls lazily upward; the fire makes you warm and drowsy, and again you lie
down—to again awaken with a sense of chilliness—to find the
fire burned low and daylight breaking. You have slept better
than you would in your own room at home. You have slept in
an 'Indian Camp'!

"You have also learned the difference between such a simple shelter and an open-air bivouac under a tree or beside an
old log."

Nessmuk's *Woodcraft*, for all its charm, dates back about 85
years, and Kephart's *Camping and Woodcraft* about 60 years.
Lots of water has gone over the dam since then.

"Except for a ten-day trip in Michigan some 90 years ago,"
Colonel Whelen told me, "the only back packing that George
W. Sears (Nessmuk) ever did was across short carries between
lakes in the Adirondacks. I met Nessmuk when I was a small

boy, came on him in a small cabin on Eagle Lake in the Adirondacks one day. I remember him as a very friendly old man.

"Kephart I knew personally and corresponded with a lot. A very fine man indeed! His was long the best book on its subject, but it is weak in parts, and Kephart did not have extended field experience. In fact, all his experience was confined to the Great Smoky Mountains in North Carolina and to some of the swampy country on the Mississippi River below St. Louis, in neither of which place could he have acquired much information on back packing, for instance. Kephart was well read, but there were relatively few books by specialists in outdoor living in his day. In Sears's time there were practically none."

As each of us observes the world from a different trail, it is only natural that points of view will vary. Take for example, three sportsmen approaching a water hole. One will see only the disappearing cubs. Another will see the large bear hurrying nearer. The third will see both cubs and mother. I do not, for a moment, suppose that my ways are the only ways, but at least it may be helpful to know the other fellow's points. Here is what I have learned from a lifetime in the farther places about building a lean-to.

BUILDING THE MOST EFFICIENT LEAN-TO

Ideally, you'll want a shelter about a foot longer than your height so that you can bask lengthwise in it alongside a long night fire. Say you have at least a good sheath knife.

First of all, you pick a level bit of land in as sheltered a place as is available. Make as sure as possible that it is in no imminent danger of falling trees, limbs, or other objects, and pull up any brush. If there is any danger of lightning, avoid lone tall trees, as these may draw bolts.

Next comes your ridgepole. Fell and smooth a sapling sufficiently long to reach between two branched trees if any are handy, between one branch in such a tree and a three-pole forked and interlocked tripod, or between two such tripods.

Conservatively, you'll want the mouth of your lean-to high enough to sit in upon browse at least one foot thick. Situate your ridgepole at the adequate height.

You'll want a shed roof slanting at about a forty-five-degree angle, one reaching to the ground at a distance wide enough to accommodate your bed if you are alone, two or three beds if you have companions. If there are more than three in your party, you'll likely want another lean-to. Do not make the common mistake of building these opposite one another so that you can share a common fire, for one or the other shelter will almost certainly be plagued with smoke.

You'll want at least one slanting back pole at each corner of the desired length, say a comfortable seven feet. Trim these so that enough branch stubs remain to support at least two horizontal poles at the back.

The temperature promises to plummet below zero before morning, so you'll want walls at least half a foot, and preferably a foot, thick. These will best be made of thickly needled conifer boughs, cut so that each end will have a stub that will hook over the desired horizontal pole. Begin at the lowest level and hook the upside down boughs, each long enough to reach the ground at the desired angle, as close together as practical. The next row will overlap these, and so on, providing a thick roof that will shed a considerable amount of rain, sleet, or snow. The wedgelike ends are no problem. Just lay a few saplings against these, upside down if the weather is stormy or threatening.

By building such a framework tighter, it can be thatched with other materials at hand, such as sod, grass, leafy branches and the like, or, at the other extreme, by palm fronds. The principle is to do the best you can with the available materials. Snow is such a good insulator that it can simplify the problem. I have spent a number of comfortable nights along far northern rivers by clearing a shelter among several shore rocks, covering one end top and bottom with browse, and building a reflecting fire in the open end. In any event, here's where you can incorporate a modern touch. Waterproof the roof with the sheet of plastic we have already recommended, anchoring it with leaning small trees or such.

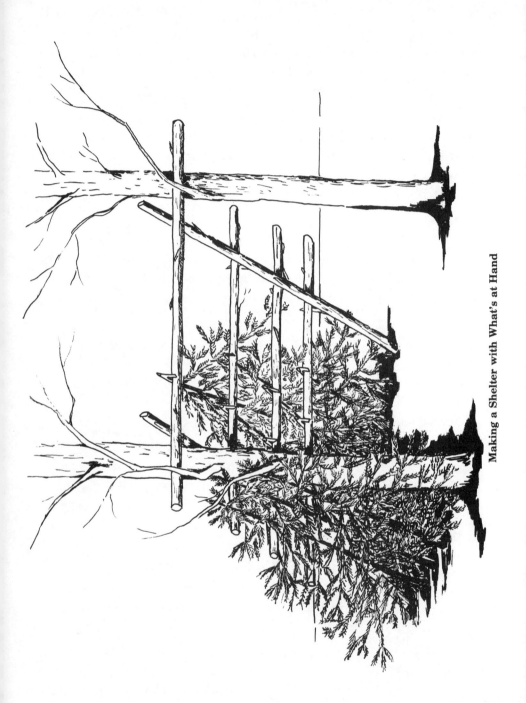

Making a Shelter with What's at Hand

Unless you have an air or foam mattress, make a browse bed (described later in this chapter), build up your body-length fire, preferably with a reflector behind it, pile up spare firewood by your head, and you'll be well away. When you rouse in the morning, you'll be rested, refreshed, and ready for whatever the trail has to offer.

SLEEPING BAG AND MATTRESS

Especially if you are traveling with watercraft or with pack animals, the handiest bed will be a sleeping bag atop an air or foam mattress. Comfort? I've slept for years on a flat surface in the heaviest obtainable 90-by-90 waterfowl down sleeping bag, leaving it open or partially so during the warmer months; not even the most expensive king-size beds in the cities have proved as comfortable.

For years I recommended snaps rather than zippers. Now the ubiquitous zipper has worked its way into virtually every piece of outerwear sold in America. This is particularly true in the matter of the sleeping bag, especially as the shells and liners of the better bags, such as the ones sold by firms like Gerry (5450 North Valley Highway, Denver, Colorado 80216), are made from lightweight nylons with which metal snaps make a poor marriage. Nylon is easily cut if the pressure on a snap-setting machine is too intense. If this happens, the snap can easily separate from the fabric the first time you try to open the snap. If the pressure is too weak, the snap will not fit snugly and will pull out in the first few weeks of use.

There have been great improvements in zippers, too. For several years now, Gerry has been using a #7 nylon coil zipper manufactured by YKK in Japan, each half of the zipper being made of a single strand of heavy-gauge nylon monofilament. This makes it virtually impossible for a tooth to break or for the material to be torn if it is inadvertently caught in the zipper. Since switching to this type of zipper, according to manager of dealer services D.W. Robinson, this Outdoor Sports Company subsidiary has "virtually eliminated returns of sleeping bags due to faulty zippers." I have personally tested this zipper, even frozen, and have discovered it to be practically foolproof. So, after years of recommending snaps over zippers, I find that another milestone has been passed.

Mattress? I personally favor an air mattress with something hard, like a strip of bark, at the head between mattress and down. The whole secret with air mattresses is to inflate them properly, the tendency being to make them too hard. Do this at first, as with the easily packed bulblike rubber pump I purchased from L. L. Bean in Freeport, Maine 04032 for a dollar forty years ago, lie on your side, and let out air through the mattress vent until your hipbone is just touching the hard surface. Then it will be precisely right. The way to find a leak in an air mattress, by the way, is to inflate it solidly and then immerse it in still water until the telltale climb of bubbles is noted. Fix by letting the fabric dry and then applying an adhesive and a small patch of rubber.

While I prefer air because of its adaptability and, to me, its

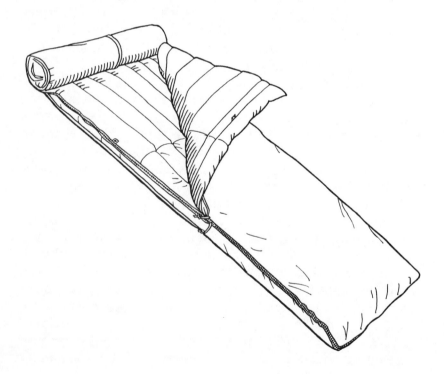

extra ease, the newer foam mattresses have proved excellent, too, and can be compressed into as small a space. They have the undeniable advantage of not needing repairs. By purchasing the best article obtainable at first, an axiom to be followed in buying all permanent backwoods gear, you'll have little if any trouble over the years.

If you are traveling extra light, either settle for an abbreviated mattress for the vulnerable hip area alone, utilizing woodland materials for the rest of the body, or use entirely what the bush has to offer. At Camp Herrick at Lake Winnipesaukee in New Hampshire, for instance, we used to build rectangles of pegged poles and fill them with dry evergreen needles. This was an improvement over my earlier camps when I'd made do by leveling a spot, kicking out as many stones and snags as possible, and then toeing or heeling out shoulder and hip holes. Not even an armful of boughs, arranged helter-skelter, could make this really comfortable, although it was adequate during those youthful adventures.

THE BROWSE BED

Then on the Half Moon of the Southwest Miramichi River in New Brunswick, where I was salmon fishing just before freezeup, I built my first browse bed after we'd trimmed camp to backpacking proportions. I've enjoyed the warm and aromatic softness of many since, always in the deep woods. The browse bed is not for camps in civilization or near the fringes of it. Nor is it for one in a hurry, for it is carefully thatched, a process requiring about half an hour.

Commence by tearing or cutting off what will at first attempt be a surprising lot of young and bushy evergreen boughs, carrying the large but light collection on a long stick at whose end has been left a branch in the form of a "V". Lay down a foot-thick layer of springy green boughs at the head, placing these upside down as you do throughout. Continue with overlapping tiers, covering the hard butts, all of which extend toward the bottom of the bed, until it is of body length. Complete by leveling with inserted tips wherever necessary.

More trips for additional boughs will likely be necessary before the thatch is about one foot in depth. The experience of such a fragrant, resilient mattress is an event every backwoodsman should try at least once. On subsequent nights you'll probably choose to rejuvenate it by poking in fresh boughs.

TENTS

Tents are very nearly necessities in the frequented places, if only for privacy. In the real backwoods it is a different matter, except when you're spending cold nights above timberline. Otherwise, not even flies or mosquitoes will make one a necessity, as you can travel with a mosquito canopy to pitch over your bed that is light enough for carrying and for good ventilation but has a mesh small enough to withstand the intrusion of even the pesky no-see-ums which appear mainly at dawn and at dusk.

The tent's principal characteristics should include resistance to storm, wind, heat or cold and—with today's usually tough, long-lived, lightweight fabrics—condensation, an especially important consideration when you realize that an individual of average size and weight emits close to 45 cubic inches of moisture per night through breathing and perspiration. For this reason, a breathable inner fabric covered with a waterproof outer fly will create a dead-air space that is several degrees warmer than the outside air, so that vaporized water from within the tent proper will escape through the walls before condensing. This is done most effectively today with a breathing inner tent and an outside waterproofed fly.

Cotton fabrics have been found to present too many problems, including weight, weakness, mildew, and rot. Nearly all quality lightweight tents today are made of nylon in two general weaves: a taffeta with a smooth texture that, being more abrasion-resistant, is suitable for flooring when it is finished with a heavy application of durable, waterproof urethane; and a breathable ripstop fabric reinforced with extra thread to help stop tearing. This is suitable as is for the usual tent proper and, when treated with the waterproof urethane, for the waterproof flies.

Such a combination tent, which functionally should be fire-resistant if only so that a spark from the campfire will not burn it as happened all too frequently with the old, paraffin-waterproofed cottons, should have seams that are well over-lapped, conscientiously sewn, and reinforced in the stress areas. A sound thread is dacron for strength, covered with a cotton that will swell when wet to fill and waterproof otherwise vulnerable needle holes. Finally, it should have a fine nylon mesh front and back for thorough ventilation and to keep out the smallest insects. This should be as darkly colored as possible, both because it makes for easier visibility and because it attracts fewer bugs. The zippers should be the ruggedest, most troublefree available.

In extreme conditions, even the best tents are plagued with

two shortcomings which, fortunately, can be handily solved. In severe cold, even tunnel vents are not sufficient to handle moisture which is always being expelled by the body and which tends to freeze upon contact. A breathable, cotton, inner frost lining can be added and removed daily for shaking out the frozen moisture, while the most substantial nylon zippers are a great improvement over the old, weaker, colder metal zippers which tended to freeze. Secondly, above the tree line you'll need implements for erecting the tent, such as poles, frames, pegs, etc. These should be light but robust aircraft-alloy aluminum pieces with extra-strength center sections to insure their reliability against heavy snow and wind.

Such a total combination, easily sleeping two individuals and rugged enough to withstand heavy weather, can be obtained in models weighing less than eight pounds. As for expense, I've proved to myself over the years that the aptest policy is to buy what, although not always the most costly by a long way, is the best. The best safeguard for the uninformed is to deal with a reputable, experienced, and trustworthy dealer. The best proof of this is that I am still using the everyday equipment that I bought when I first took to the woods.

PITCHING YOUR TENT

When pitching your tent, look for a dry, smooth, level spot with, preferably, a good view. Halfway down the lee side of a slope will be the warmest. Get as near a good water source as practical without subjecting yourself, in season, to too much humidity and too many insects. Respect, of course, the usual safety factors.

Getting the floor of the tent square and not too taut is well worth the extra time and trouble it will take. As you proceed, put a little tension evenly on the guy ropes. If you are using a fly, make sure that this does not sag and rub on the tent itself, as this can cause leakage and wear. Naturally, keep the highly vulnerable fabric free from sharp or abrasive objects. Finally, sponging the fabric with warm water and mild soap and wiping the pegs and such clean will make for a longer and pleasanter tent life.

TARPAULIN

An eight-by-ten, lightweight, waterproof, fire-retardant tarpaulin is often all one needs in the forested backwoods in reasonably temperate weather, particularly since, if it is rugged, it will have a number of functional uses other than that of a shelter.

One can be pitched many ways but, except in the stormiest weather, I usually put up mine with a horizontal ridgepole as a simple lean-to, with the sides bushed in by leaning small live conifers or any leafy brush against them. This way you can cook and sleep comfortably in all but the roughest weather. During the latter, pitch the tarp as a tent with the openings enclosed by brush, preferably small conifers leaned upside down to better shed the rain, sleet, or snow, and cook as best you can in a sheltered spot nearby, perhaps under a safe ledge or large tree.

The thin, lightweight, eight-by-ten sheet of plastic, durable enough that I have not had to replace mine in three decades and no more bulky than a folded handkerchief, I use the same as a tarp for day-to-day travel, but of course it cannot stand a really hard blow or be used as ground cloth.

A basic rule-of-thumb is to have your shelter's opening back to the wind. In open country in cold weather, however, drifts will be built up by the wind in front of your abode, blocking the exit. In these conditions, the best procedure is to place the entrance at right angles to the wind. This is also the best compromise when you are bedding down in a chasm, probably by a mountain stream where you are getting your water, where the thermal air currents vary with the time. In stormy weather, as every hunter knows, these currents drift upward in the early morning and then ebb downward at the approach of evening. If you are located in flattish terrain for an indefinite length of time, the placing of your shelter's exit and entrance should be determined by the prevailing wind, which can be determined by the leaning of the trees and usually by the direction of the windfall.

THE WHELEN LEAN-TO TENT

I have always loved the primitive wilderness for itself, not to shut myself away from it in a closed tent. For that reason, when traveling back of beyond where weight is not a factor, as by canoe or horse, I have always used a so-called Whelen Lean-To Tent, designed by my late writing companion and successor to Nessmuk and Kephart, Colonel Townsend Whelen. As a result of such Army assignments as director of research and development at the Springfield Armory, commanding officer at the Frankfort Arsenal, and ordnance representative on the Infantry Board, experimentation in attaining maximum performance came to be second nature to my friend, who thought up what he modestly called a Hunter's Lean-To Tent. It has been marketed without financial gain to him by a number of manufacturers over the years and most recently by the Colorado Tent and Awning Company, 3333 East 52nd Avenue, Denver, Colorado 80216.

The Whelen Lean-To has a canopy under which you can cook in a rainstorm. The sides are ideally suited for heat reflection and additional room, for they angle outward and forward at the bottom some two feet from where a weighted cord would touch the ground if suspended from the ends of the six-foot-wide ridge. With this, the walls angle at such a pitch that, besides reflecting heat and light into the shelter, the frontal extension hinders wind and breezes from making the front sanctuary chilly while at the same time affording storage room for personal belongings near the head of the sleeping bag. The cooking gear and foodstuffs can be stored at the foot. Because there is only a single slanting wall in back, both the expense and the difficulty of construction is lessened, while pitching is made easier. Additional room for storage is also provided, usually even when two individuals sleep side-by-side and parallel to the front.

Loops extend above the six-foot tape ridge to hold the ridgepole. Under this tape ridge are two additional loops to

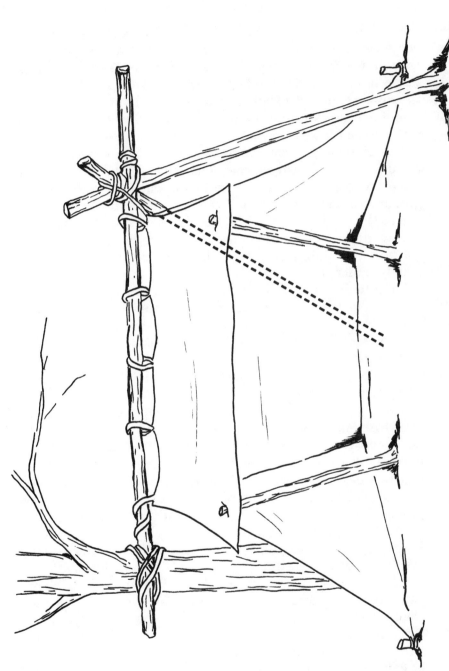

Whelen Lean-to Tent

hold a short pole on which clothing can be hung for convenience or for drying. An awning is sewed to the ridge. Although it is easiest to toss this backward over the ridgepole in warm fair weather, it can be extended forward and downward to provide additional shelter in front, to help prevent a storm from hurling itself into the tent, and to create a covered area under which to sit and cook.

Troublesome guy ropes over which one is always tripping are unnecessary. Instead, sharpen both ends of a pair of poles some six feet long. Extend one end of each through the big grommet at each outer end of the awning. Implant the other end at the head and foot of the sleeping bag, thus maintaining the awning taut some four feet above the forest floor where warmth and illumination from the long fire in front will beat snugly under it.

For pitching the Whelen Lean-To Tent, merely cut and trim a slim ridgepole perhaps a dozen feet in length, long enough to extend between the branches of handy trees or to be held some six feet high by shear poles. Then just stake down the sides and backs, and your shelter is ready.

The sides, splayed as suggested, will do a great deal to keep smoke from being drawn inside the shelter and, indeed, will do away with this annoyance almost completely if you build your fire against a large rock or safe ledge or slant a tier of back logs at least a foot high against green poles behind the blaze. This will make the tent the snuggest and coziest living quarters easily available back of beyond. With an adequate sleeping bag you'll need no night fire except for the cheery blaze you'll want to dream in front of until it's time to turn in; without even getting out of your bag, you can have tinder, kindling, and wood available for building the morning fire for breakfast and for getting the kinks out of your muscles.

If flying pests are around, merely pitch on small poles above your head an easily available, inexpensive mosquito bar, small-meshed enough to prevent even the intrusion of no-see-ums. And before you leave its sanctuary, douse yourself with a good repellent. In really cold weather, insulate the air or foam mattress beneath you with browse, then keep a rousing fire going all night.

Colonel Whelen gave me permission to pass along his long-proved design if you'd like the easy and pleasurable adventure of building such a shelter yourself for the fun of it, for economy, and perhaps because such a commercial tent may no longer be easily available.

Waterproof ripstop nylon, bought coated with urethane and weighing 2.5 ounces per square yard, may be purchased at a cost of $3.30 a square yard at this writing from The Ski Hut at 1615 University Avenue, Berkeley, California 94701. With the findings, your Whelen Lean-To Tent will weigh about 3.5 pounds. Suitable material is also available from other catalog-mailing companies advertising in the large outdoor magazines. The key details are shown in the illustration on page 54.

CARBON MONOXIDE

There may be times—as when you're mountain climbing above timberline, sleeping and cooking in a closed tent where mosquitoes are thick enough to kill anyone unprotected from them, camping in such cold that it would take too long to accumulate the wood for a body-length fire and you're using instead perhaps a Sims folding stove, or when in deep wilderness you come across an abandoned prospector's or trapper's shack that is too handy to pass by—when you should take into account carbon monoxide, which is a peril in any closed space where there is combustion of any kind, even the motor vehicle which is carrying you to the jumping-off spot.

Carbon monoxide, the always existing and vital carbon dioxide with a single atom of oxygen missing, is the everyday byproduct of incomplete combustion. Carbon monoxide is so avid for that absent particle of oxygen that it will seize it at the earliest possible moment from whatever is at hand. If this is the blood, it can be hazardous if not lethal. Carbon monoxide is especially hazardous because it is both invisible and impossible to smell and, even more insidiously, because its effects build up in the body until just one more breath can

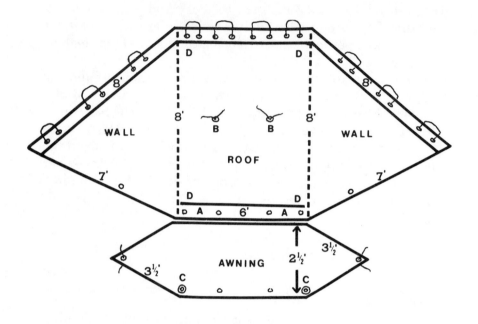

Pattern for Whelen Lean-to Tent

overcome the victim. Like scurvy, it has killed more outdoorsmen than will ever be known.

In the woods, carbon monoxide commonly becomes fatal before one is aware of it. There is no difficulty in breathing. In
an enclosed place, one may become alerted by the fact that a
candle or lantern starts to lose its brightness, but what generally happens is that the victim is so suddenly stricken that
before he comprehends that something is awry, he is almost, if
not entirely, immobile. In a closed tent whose fabric is sealed
by waterproofing or by frost, rain, or snow, a heater as tiny as
a primus stove can, and on numerous unrealized occasions
has, killed the occupants.

Symptoms of carbon monoxide poisoning, if one becomes
alerted to them as one may be in a cumulative situation, start

with tautness across the forehead, headache, and a redness in the complexion. The headache becomes increasingly annoying with continued exposure to the gas. Then comes debility, giddiness, failing sight, indigestion and possible vomiting, and finally helplessness and unconsciousness.

If one is alone, the only possible remedy is somehow to get fresh air, as by slitting a canvas, breaking a window, or crawling into the open. If the weather is cold, there will be the added danger of freezing unless one can somehow manage to drag a sleeping bag with him. Rest is the rule to decrease ordinary oxygen requirements in breathing and warmth to lessen the amount of oxygen needed by the tissues.

If there is help, begin mouth-to-mouth resuscitation at once. This is preferable to other personal methods of forced breathing because of the small amount of carbon dioxide in the breath. In fact, if several unaffected individuals will take deep breaths, exhale into a container, such as a plastic bag, and have the patient take similarly deep breaths of the stored air, the effects of the carbon monoxide impregnation may be cured in half an hour rather than the several hours otherwise necessary.

An unconscious camper who has been exposed to the gas as in fires and smoke, and whose skin, tongue and interior of the mouth, and tissue under the fingernails are bright red, may be assumed to be a victim of carbon monoxide poisoning. To prevent it, make certain of adequate circulation of fresh air at all times, no matter where you may be.

SERENITY

I for one, unless circumstances intervene, don't go into the deep wilderness to shut myself away from the some two thousand stars we can see with the naked eyes, from the spacious view, nor to miss the joy of a campfire—and the memorable luxury of hunching up in the morning and getting breakfast started, with the glory of the east, whenever possible, and the country I am going to hunt, fish, prospect, or explore that day quickening before me.

CHAPTER 4

Heat and Cold

Staying warm or keeping cool, whichever difficulty besets you at the moment, is the third most important challenge in successfully living, which includes enjoying yourself, in any remote region. Once you have proved to your own inner satisfaction that you can take, with the barest possible minimum of gear, whatever the elments have to offer, you come to realize—the wiser you are the quicker—that the real requirement is learning to smooth it. After all, we get it rough enough in the ever tightening tentacles of civilization.

COLD-WEATHER CAMPING

When wraiths of mist, which the Hudson's Bay Company men call the ghosts of departed voyageurs, began coursing down the Peace River the first winter I stayed in the Subarctic Forest, I was ready for hibernation. Oatmeal sacks, both for my pack dog and myself, bulged plumply in the newly readied cache by my log cabin. Moose quarters, marbled with fat, promised many a steak and savory roast. Glancing through the whiteness at stacks of split poplar and lodgepole pine, I stirred my cookstove fire with more satisfaction than ever.

I wasn't planning to get very far outdoors in weather so frigid that an individual's spittle was reputed to congeal between mouth and ground and if, when lost, you stopped walking around a tree all night, they'd have to sharpen your frozen body to drive it into the earth to bury it. Besides, what about drinking water? Everything would be thick with snow, and I'd heard that snow is something a thirsty man should shy away from for, besides making him more parched than ever, it's for some reason downright hazardous to eat in cold weather.

Of course, I didn't go for that frozen saliva legend. This would require more than a 60° temperature drop between lips and the ground. As for the other things, well, like most of us, I'd been hearing them all my life, along with what passes as other cold-weather lore. Such as how to thaw a frostbitten ear by rubbing it with snow, and about shoving a frozen foot into some cold liquid like kerosene that's been kept outdoors. And about bundling up in lots of heavy clothing to stay alive when the colored alcohol in the thermometer falls an inch or more below zero; and how if you fall asleep on a log in such cold, you're not going to awaken this side of paradise.

Dangerous is something cold-weather camping very definitely is not. This kind of venture is in many ways actually the most comfortable and pleasant you can enjoy. There are no troublesome insects, and the litterbugs and ribbon clerks are back where the steam heat is sizzling.

The wilderness is wide open. There's a wonderfully lonesome wail to the wind. You can see everything that's going on around you during this marvelously unobstructed time of year. Not only that, but at your feet is tracked the record of what has happened not long before. To have a good time, though, you've got to go at it the right way, but that's easy. Let's have a look at some of the honest facts.

SNOW

One of the very real luxuries of the winter outdoors is that a drink of water is as near as your hand. As you prospect, track, or progress along, you can at any time scoop up a handful of snow. The only precaution that need be taken is to treat it like ice cream and not put down too much when you're overheated or chilled. Aside from that, clean snow can be safely eaten whenever you are thirsty in the bush.

Dangerous? Why? Wilderness snows, after all, afford in flake form the purest of distilled water from the atmosphere. The only disadvantage is that it takes a lot to equal even a small amount of water. This drawback is more than made up for, though, by the fact that snowfall makes water quickly available through the wild places, an invaluable advantage inasmuch as we need a lot more water in freezing weather than one might suppose—at least two quarts a day—for the kidneys then have to take over much of the process of eliminating waste materials otherwise handled by the sweat glands. Snow used for drinking water, far from being harmful, is therefore an extremely healthful convenience.

FROSTBITE

The same sort of good judgment can be applied to the widely reiterated nonsense that the way to thaw a frozen ear is to rub it with snow. First of all, thawing frozen flesh by friction is apt to compound the damage by tearing the sensitized area. Second, rubbing the ear with snow under such conditions is like reaching up right now and scrubbing it with gravel.

To thaw a frozen ear on the trail, press a warm hand over it. To thaw a frostbitten finger, shove it under a warm armpit. To thaw a foot that has started to freeze, usually a totally unnecessary emergency, build a fire if you can do so quickly. Otherwise, keeping as well covered as you can, hold it against a warm part of the body, such as directly against the bare thigh. If a companion is with you, the thing to do, if he will agree, is to thrust it against his bare abdomen. The warm body cavity of a freshly killed animal can also afford a solution.

Don't ever make the terrible error of trying to thaw a part of the body by immersing it in a liquid such as oil or gasoline that has been stored at subzero temperatures. Although far colder than 32°F, these and other fluids have sometimes been used in the disastrous belief that because they were not fro-

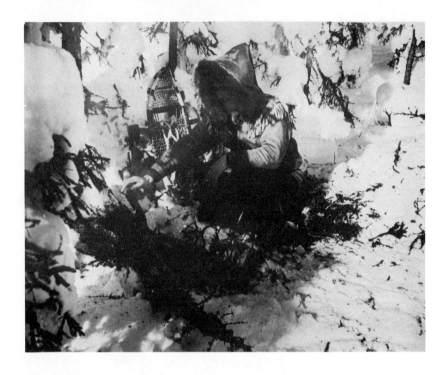

zen, they were just the things to use to painlessly thaw something else.

Freezing, like every potential danger in the wilderness, isn't actually much of a threat to an experienced individual except as it may result from accidents. Against these we habitually take simple but ample precautions. Our own inbred ingenuity and resourcefulness, stimulated by the instinct for survival, care for the rest. Besides, as has been said, a man sits as many risks as he runs.

Among the many prospectors, trappers, sportsmen, outfitters, loggers, and other outdoorsmen among whom I've lived for years, often in primitive wilderness where the population averages less than one human for every dozen square miles and where temperatures fall 100°F below freezing, no one I know personally has ever been incapacitated or even seriously bothered by freezing. Do you know what's really the greatest cause of accidental death in the snowy regions? Another case of opposites: it's not cold at all, but fire.

KEEPING WARM

"Bundle up in lots of heavy clothes. It's cold outside," may be good advice for the city, but it's another thing that can kill you in the Far North. An error to avoid, no matter what, is the extremely common mistake on the part of the newcomer of dressing too warmly in subzero weather. Excessive sweating should be avoided by every reasonable means during the northern frigidity, if only because it undermines insulation efficiency. The amount of sweating that goes on at all times is heightened by clothing that is warmer than necessary. If the garments do not allow sufficient ease of movement and if they are not unrestricting enough to permit the escape of this dampness, the perspiration can freeze inside the garb in subzero weather. The consequence will be, at the very least, uncomfortable; at worst, it can lessen the amount of insulation enough to kill you.

It is therefore imperative that on those days when one needs a twelve-inch thermometer with zero at the top, he should avoid sweating too profusely. All this is a major reason why, for the typical outdoorsman, the layer system is best in cold country. In the morning chill, which actually deepens at sunrise because of the breezes stirred by the lifting of the sun, many like to leave camp wearing everything reasonable. Whether on the tundra or high in the mountains, the practice is to continue shedding layers of clothing as the sun soars higher and storing them in a packsack. It is always best to anticipate personal warmth variations, to open clothing before you'd otherwise begin to sweat, and to close it again before you actually feel chilly.

The neatest undercover trick for cold-country comfort lies in some of the recently developed insulative underwear. You should still don net underwear next to your skin, however; ideally, this should be ⅜ of an inch or larger square mesh, about ⅛ inch thick, and entirely open like a fishnet. Much smaller holes, as well as the familiar waffle-weave undersuits, do not permit the necessary evaporation to take place.

No matter what you wear, the garments as a whole should be sufficient to give you an average thickness that will be adequate according to both temperature and your particular rate of metabolism. With correctly designed cold-weather clothing and the best of the new down or synthetic underwear, you can wear your maximum thickness throughout the day and ventilate any excess heat from inside it.

When you find that you are wearing too much at the moment, uncover that most efficient heat radiator you have, your head. If this isn't enough, open your neck and, if necessary, your front to let out the heat accumulating at the torso. The wrists and hands are next on the ventilating scale. The veins that are closest to the surface on the underneath of your wrist make these effective radiators. In addition, by permitting air to move up the arms, you are cooling the armpits which are one of the foremost heat-producing regions of the human system.

The final source of ventilation is the legs. The general practice, often necessary because of deep snow, it to leave them very lightly insulated. Although this generally works, it increases the tendency toward cold feet by dropping the blood temperature as it travels down the exposed limbs—the solution to which may be two sets of heavy woolen socks and a pair of lightweight thermal boots.

FALLING ASLEEP AND FREEZING

One of the commonest and most dangerous of the many false notions surrounding the subject of cold-weather camping is the persistent notion that if caught out overnight in very cold weather, you shouldn't let yourself fall asleep, or you'll freeze and never awaken.

That chestnut, which a good many people took the trouble to pass along when they heard I was going to live in the North Woods, had me so apprehensive for awhile that I found myself not caring even to relax too comfortably on a log during the day for more than a couple of minutes. When you stop to think it over, however, you'll see as I did, and as I went to the trouble of personally proving for the good of my soul, that the precise opposite is true.

To put it briefly, passing over the obvious effects to be expected from excessive perspiring and from exhaustion, the only way the human system can manufacture the warmth needed to offset cold is by burning calories. The reserve of these energy units readily available for this need will be greatly lessened if, as many advise, we consume them by aimlessly hiking around a tree all night.

The ideal, if you are caught out unprepared, is to get a campfire going and then to lie on something waterproof between it and its reflected warmth. The next best procedure is to hole up while dry and fresh in as sheltered a spot as you can find, to curl or hunch on something such as bark or boughs, and to relax.

If you do fall asleep, the increasing coldness will finally awaken you. You may stir around just enough to get warm, which is frequently all one does at home, and then relax again and maybe grab another strength-conserving nap. From a perspiration-chilled sleep of exhaustion that too many times is the result of trying to keep going, there is often no awakening.

Cold-weather camping lives longer in our memories than most done in the milder seasons, as I confirmed that first northern year and reaffirmed during many afterward.

DESERT ACCLIMATIZATION

The low humidity in desert country is an advantage in that it makes the body seem cooler by evaporating the moisture that is always being excreted through your pores, even when you do not seem to be perspiring. It is a disadvantage in that you need more water to continue this function and, even though you do not seem to be thirsty, you should continue to drink small amounts of water frequently.

To keep body heat at its lowest and thus conserve this water, wear loose, light-colored clothing, which will reflect the heat better, and a wide-brimmed hat, preferably with a chin strap so that it will not be blown off and dangerously lost. Again, a light-colored hat reflects the heat more efficiently. A high crown, not fashionably dented, provides functional air space. Ventilation, provided by air holes in the crown near the top, is very helpful. Although a straw hat passes the test for ventilation, it will give no protection from wind and infrequent rain, nor will it long withstand the necessary rigors to which it must be subjected. In any event, keep the head covered from the bludgeoning sun, even if this covering is only fabric or extra clothing held in place as securely as necessary by a lace or cord.

It has been proved that a fully clothed individual will remain cooler than one who is only partially clothed. This may be extended to sleeves, although, like everything else, they should be loose and as well ventilated as possible. Avoid, too, coming into any more contact than necessary with hot objects and seek shade whenever possible.

As the U. S. Air Force recommends, "Take a lesson from the Arab. He is not *surviving* on the desert. He lives there and likes it. He isn't lazy. He's just living in slow motion, the way

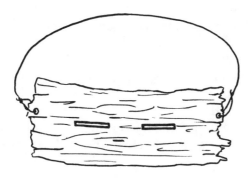

Improvised Sunglasses

the desert makes him live." Slow and steady, in other words, does it on a hot desert. When you move about in the heat, you'll last longer on less water if you take it easy.

It is the custom among desert inhabitants to keep their tents open on all sides during the light of the day to permit free circulation of air. Sit or lie a few inches above the rocks and sand if this is at all possible, for it can be 30° to 40° cooler above the desert floor.

SUNGLASSES IN THE DESERT

Sunglasses are such a necessity against the glare that, in a pinch, you should make substitutes by slitting bark or fabric and holding them in place by a cord around the temples and the back of the head. As far as seeing is concerned, if you are unaccustomed to desert travel, triple your estimates of distance, as both the clear dry air and the relative absence of terrain features are apt to make under-estimations probable.

DESERT FOOTWEAR

Although you will be avoiding loose sand and rough terrain whenever possible, which requires following the hard valleys or ridges among sand dunes, care of your feet is essential. In a pinch, you can cross sand dunes barefoot in cool weather, but during the summer the sand will burn your feet.

Dependable low boots with composition soles, the same that are recommended for general travel in chapter 8, are a necessity. Hard leather is slippery on the rocky desert and, as if this were not enough, wears out too quickly. For short excursions only, rubber-soled sneakers, preferably one of the ankle-supporting and -protecting varieties, will do. So, too, will the rubber-soled leather boot when laced loosely so that the air will squish in and out. The usual high-heeled western cowboy boots are, among other shortcomings, too slippery.

SANDSTORM PROTECTION

If a sandstorm should blow up, take shelter at the earliest possible moment. Mark your direction with an arrow of stones, lie down with your back to the gale, cover your nose and mouth with a cloth, and try to sleep through the spectacle.

If possible, seek shelter in the lee of a hill. Don't worry about being buried by the sand. In fact, it's recommended that when necessary you get some protection from the sun by covering your body with sand. Too, burrowing in the sand also reduces water loss, while its pressure affords valuable physical relief to tired muscles.

In extreme situations, if at all possible scoop out an east-west trench several feet deep, as the temperature at the bottom of this may be as much as a dramatic 100° lower than that on the desert floor. A shovel should be in your outfit for desert travel.

GLOVES IN THE DESERT

Because nearly everything on the desert is sharp, pointed, thorny, rough, dusty, or hot, a pair of heavy, flexible, and preferably leather gloves that are stout enough to withstand cacti are pretty much a must.

COLD ON THE DESERT

Especially on the high North American deserts, it can get downright cold when the sun goes below the horizon, and a

fleecy woolen shirt or, preferably, a lightweight down jacket will be needed. If goosedown encased in nylon is selected, the garment will be both more versatile and warmer in relation to weight.

Elastic knit cuffs are effective to seal off the wrist openings, and a hooded top, even when the hood is not used, is warmer about the neck. Without it, I would substitute a small woolen scarf. For utmost efficiency in warmth, use a waist belt.

Lightweight nylon fabrics and metal snaps tend to tear loose. Although I formerly was a staunch supporter of snaps on all outdoor wear, I have used one of the improved nylon zippers on my Gerry jacket for several years. Each half of the zipper is made of a single strand of heavy-gauge monofilament, making it virtually impossible for a tooth to break or for the material to be torn if it is accidentally caught in the mechanism.

CHAPTER 5

Then Comes Water

Water is the next most important necessity no matter where you are. With other conditions being favorable, you can live for a month or more without food, although as we'll consider later this is seldom necessary. Yet even under the best of circumstances, you would be lucky to stay alive for much more than about a week without water. Fortunately, water, too, is nearly everywhere.

It used to be that we didn't think much about the water we drank in the wilderness, just so long as it was clear and sparkling and, preferably, cool. But now we know that purity is not guaranteed by getting back of beyond. Even the primitive beaver, which originally lured the mountainmen west and was an important factor in opening the North American continent, is a carrier of tularemia which, although modern antibiotics can control it if you can get to them, can make one very sick indeed.

I'll never forget the day that I was exploring a canyon in northern British Columbia where probably no human being had been since the stampede to the Klondike gold strikes at the turn of the century and where certainly one might have expected that no water could be more pure than the crystalline little stream that trickled down its middle. I boiled the kettle as usual and enjoyed my noonday H.B.C. Fort Garry black tea to sluice down moose kabobs and peanut butter and wild raspberry jam sandwiches made with sourdough bread that Vena had baked the day before. And was I ever glad about the boiling when a couple of hundred yards further along, where the canyon dwindled to steep, narrow rapids which I ascended by climbing through the stream, now narrow enough on the plateau above to leap, I found the body of a decomposing moose. In other words, we can never be too careful anywhere.

BEST WAYS TO PURIFY WATER

There is a best way to purify drinking water and all water used for such personal tasks as brushing teeth and for cooking in which high heat is not a factor. Boil the water for five minutes at sea level, one additional minute for each 1000 feet of elevation.

Formerly, one could do a pretty safe job in the North with Halazone tablets, and we still can if we want to spend, at this writing, something like three dollars for what used to be a forty-cent bottle of the tiny chlorine-releasing pellets. Iodine water purification tablets, necessary in warm and tropical climates for similar use, cost even more.

It's too bad, for both are easy to use. A pair of Halazone tablets can ordinarily be depended upon in temperate climates to make a quart of water pure enough for human consumption in half an hour. If the water seems particularly dangerous or if it's muddy, use four Halazone tablets and leave them in for an hour.

All parts of the container with which the water will later come in contact must, of course also be sterilized. Say you're using a one-quart canteen. Fill it, drop in the Halazone, cap loosely, and wait for five minutes. Then shake the contents so vigorously that some of the water will splash over the top, lid, and lips of the canteen. Tighten the cap and let stand for the desirable time.

The U.S. Government found out a few years ago that compounds that release chlorine gas cannot be relied upon for water purification in hot country. Necessary in such regions is something such as the iodine water purification tablets manufactured as Globaline by WTS Pharmaceuticals, Division of Wallace and Tiernan, Inc., Rochester, New York 14625. Any drugstore can secure these for you, although most pharmacists will probably have to do some looking.

Like Halazone, these tablets must be kept dry. The container, therefore, should be tightly capped as soon as possible after opening. Directions for use are:

1. Add one tablet to a quart of clear water in container with cap, two tablets if not clear;

2. Replace cap loosely and wait five minutes;

3. Shake well, allowing a little water to leak out to disinfect the screw threads before tightening container cap;

4. Wait ten minutes before using for any purpose and, if the water is very cold, wait ten more minutes.

By the way, don't heed the hopefuls anywhere who assert that a high-proof alcoholic beverage will automatically make the accompanying water and ice harmless.

Aside from the present prices, additional disadvantages of Halazone are slow solubility and a short life of five months when stored in temperatures as warm as 89.6°F. At the temperature to be anticipated when left in your automobile's glove compartment on a summer day, 122°F, the effectiveness is cut fifty percent. Furthermore, Halazone loses three-fourths of its activity when exposed to air for two days, which gives you some idea of what happens during the frequent opening and closing of the container to get tablets.

Globaline, more stable, still loses one-fifth of its power when kept in sealed bottles for half a year at 167°F. Its initial potency lessens one-third when exposed to the air for four days.

The best, and at the same time least costly, method of chemically disinfecting camp water is with iodine. Eight drops of reasonably fresh two percent tincture of iodine, used as the tablets above, will replace Globaline adequately and won't break your budget. Only individuals with a definite sensitivity to iodine will risk any ill effects. Too, if you have ever been treated for hyperthyroidism, get your physician's approval before using any such water disinfectant. The alternative is usually not chlorination but boiling.

In extreme cases in remote regions anywhere, boiling, not chlorination, is the answer. The problem of the traveler is different from that of the municipality where, with constant testing, so-called breakpoint chlorination can be practiced where the addition of sufficient chlorine to the supply binds with its organic materials while leaving a sufficient residue of free chlorine. Even in such a renowned world capital as Paris, where breakthrough chlorination was not practiced, enteroviruses were found in the chlorinated public water. Infectious hepatitis, for example, is then a threat.

The use of crystals of elemental iodine, obtainable from your pharmacist, is the most palatable and effective way to disinfect, important because most streams in even the remotest parts of this country are now known to be polluted. The sole equipment needed for iodination with crystalline iodine is a one-ounce clear glass bottle with a leak-proof bakelite cap, containing four to eight grams, or any small quantity, of USP grade resublimed iodine, I₂.

The bottle is filled with water, capped, shaken hard for about a minute, then held upright to allow the heavy iodine crystals to drop to the bottom. These crystals are not to be used directly. Disinfection is effected at 77° by the addition of 2.5 teaspoonfuls of the near-saturated iodine solution to one quart of water for fifteen minutes. The action can be safely repeated almost a thousand times without renewing the iodine crystals, and the shelf life of crystalline iodine is limitless. Under usual conditions, a teaspoonful of the iodine solution to a quart of water, allowed to stand for forty minutes, will provide satisfactory taste and effective disinfection. If the water is murky, particularly cold, or suspected of being heavily contaminated, the concentration of the iodine solution may be increased to four teaspoonfuls with a contact time of twenty minutes.

A clear glass bottle is suggested for the procedure to allow observation of the iodine crystals. Any plastic bottles I have used have eventually taken on a brown stain. Too, plastic bottles are prone to leak as one climbs to high altitudes, then to distort and crack as one descends toward sea level.

HOW TO SOFTEN HARD WATER

The water in some regions on this continent is what you might consider to be so *hard* that, until you get used to it, indigestion may result unless you drink only small amounts at one time. Here is another instance in which boiling can be of assistance, as some of the hardening compounds are then solidified and thus avoided, the reason for heavily encrusted teakettles in such areas. Or use rain water or melted snow when possible.

HOW TO CLEAR MUDDY WATER

In numerous wilderness areas, principally where cutbanks are being eroded, the water is so muddy as to be unpleasant.

There the solution by rivermen, where bulk and weight are not problems, is to carry a barrel of clear water. There are also several other ways around the problem.

If the muddy water is left standing in a container, gravity may clear it. Another method is to pour the water into a container through sand held in a cloth. In the South, a handy portable filter is easily contrived by first stuffing one end of a three-foot section of bamboo with fresh grass, then filling the remainder of the hollow with sand. The easiest solution, and one that works more often than not, is to scoop a hole several feet back from the body of water and dip from it the water that seeps in. A sandy beach, where available, is best for this process. It must be realized, of course, that such filters will not do away with any dissolved minerals or impurities. The water, however crystalline, should still be purified. Incidentally, water that a resident finds harmless may not be such for the unaccustomed newcomer.

POISONOUS WATER HOLES

Although poisonous water holes have never been found in the remote regions north of the Canadian border, there is a scattering of sources in our southwestern deserts in which such dissolved poisons as arsenic are present. Boiling or the use of chlorine or iodine will, of course, have no effect on this. The soundest general rule is to avoid any long-established water holes around which green plants are not flourishing. Another tipoff may be the bones of unfortunate birds and animals.

WATERBAGS

In a hot climate, water can be cooled to a more pleasant temperature by using one of the waterbags that are porous enough for a little fluid to seep out and wet the outside, where it evaporates and so lowers the inner temperature. The water can be purified at the same time by adding the necessary iodination.

TIPS ON BOILING SNOW WATER

While boiling the kettle at noon in snow country, special caution must be exercised not to burn the utensil. Snow acts like a blotter. It is not enough to scoop a can full of snow and hang it over the campfire. Small amounts should be melted at first, while stirring with a clean stick, until a safe several inches of fluid protects the bottom of the container. Then begin filling the can with the snow necessary to fill your container.

You will quickly learn to break off any bits of available crust or to use the more concentrated granular snow from former storms. Best is ice or the grainlike snow found in permanent drifts in high country.

WATER FROM VEGETATION

The possibilities of obtaining water from vegetation are many, including the discovery of trapped rain. In the American tropics, for example, the branches of large trees often support air plants, relatives of the toothsome pineapple, whose thickly growing and frequently overlapping leaves catch and retain rain. It is a good idea to strain this through a clean piece of cloth to eliminate blown or fallen debris and insects. Be wary when climbing, too, to avoid such critters as ants and snakes.

In the temperate and northern regions of this continent, the sap from such trees as the maple and birch is both refreshing and nourishing. The Indians used to gash V-shaped cuts in the lower trunks of these and similar trees, such as the hickory, and insert in their points spouts which they fashioned by pushing the poisonous pith out of elderberry limbs.

Vines are good sources of water in the tropics, although unless you know what you're doing, you should never drink from a vine whose sap is milky. Otherwise, choose a large vine and lop off an easily handled length, perhaps as long as you are tall. Make the first cut at the top, as you'll already have done. Sharpen the lower end and hold your mouth or a container under it. The water will be pure and fresh.

An even easier method is to cut a deep notch in a vine as high as you can reach, sever the vine close to the ground, and let the water drip into your mouth or a container. When the water stops flowing, cut another section off the top, repeating this until the supply of fluid is exhausted.

Bamboo shoots also often have water in their hollow joints. Try shaking the stems of old, yellowish bamboo. If you detect a gurgling, cut a notch at the base of each joint and catch the water.

Only in a very genuine emergency, look to the disappearing barrel cactus of the Southwest for water. To secure this, lop off the top of the cactus and macerate the pulp in the standing portion as thoroughly as possible. Again, don't do this for an experiment or for the fun of it, for the day may come when it may save someone's life. A barrel cactus some four feet tall

First Step in Obtaining Water from a Barrel Cactus

will give five pints of refreshing, milky juice. It is preferable to scoop and press this out. You might also suck the juice from a hole cut in the plant as low as you can reach with your mouth or a container. When traveling, you can also cut the pulp into chunks and take them along to suck on when it may again prove necessary.

No cactus is poisonous, so other cacti may also give emergency drinking water if you squeeze and mash parts of them. But, again, don't try this except in a dire emergency.

THE COCONUT PALM

The coconut palm, so abundant in tropical America, furnishes both water and food. In an emergency, you may even use for sustenance the large terminal bud of the palm, usually referred to as the cabbage because of size, appearance, and shape. This delicacy, which is delicious raw or cooked, has been called Millionaire's Salad because its removal kills that particular tree.

Fallen coconuts germinate where they lie. In these, both milk and meat are consumed in the process, but the cavity is filled with a spongy mass which is called the bread. This is very sustaining either raw or roasted over the campfire, with the shell itself the handiest of containers. Even the little sprouts can be enjoyed like celery.

The young coconuts grow in clusters near the top of the palm whose slim and slippery trunk may be very difficult to climb. The answer to this problem can be a so-called climbing bandage—a dependable belt or rope that is a bit longer than the circumference of the tree. Fix this around the trunk, leaving enough room so that you can step on it with both feet. The loop on the other side of the trunk will support your weight as you reach up and grasp the trunk with both arms. Pull yourself along, doubling your knees and sliding the bandage up to a higher position with your feet. Then straighten, resting your weight on the loop while achieving a higher position. By repeating this process, you can climb to any height.

When you get them down, you'll find the nut is encased in a husk composed of a smooth exterior except for a matting of tough fibers. When you have an ax, machete, hatchet, or heavy knife, you need not remove the husk of the green coconut to drink the liquid. Whittle the husk at the top, not

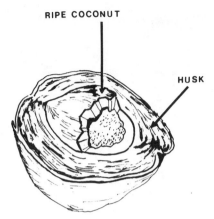

RIPE COCONUT

HUSK

Cross-Section of Coconut

the stem end, to a rough point. Then cut off the point and the top of the nut inside.

If you haven't a tool, drive into the ground a stake three or four feet long so that it slants slightly away from you. Give the top of this stake a crude, wedge-shaped edge so that it can pierce the longitudinal fibers of the husk. Stand about a foot from the stake, trying to judge a point of entry that will clear the nut within the husk. Then press the whole firmly downward against the sharpened stake with both hands, giving the coconut a twisting motion to pry off a small part of the husk. By repeating this procedure, you can remove the entire husk from either a green or a mature nut.

Once the coconut is free of the husk, the problem becomes one of breaking through the hard shell. To open a nut, hold it in one hand so that the stem-end eyes are uppermost. Using the master hand, strike it sharply just below each eye with a stone or with the point of a mature nut. The shell will crack, whereupon it will be possible to pick off the top of the nut without spilling the milk. Green coconuts give more milk than ripe ones. With a mature nut, just poke out the eyes and drink the liquid.

Incidentally, be careful not to drink more than three or four cups of ripe coconut juice a day, as it is a drastic laxative. You get over a quart of cool fluid from one young nut, especially at

How to Husk a Coconut

the jelly stage when the meat is soft. A ripe nut will gurgle when you shake it, but do not drink from very young or very old nuts.

THE BANANA TRUNK

The banana or plantain trunk of tropical and subtropical America can be made into an excellent source of water with a few cuts from a knife, machete, hatchet, or ax. Cut down the tree, leaving approximately three inches of the trunk protruding from the ground. Hollow out a bowl-like basin in this section of trunk.

Water will immediately flow into this reservoir from the roots. This fluid will taste bitter, but if the bowl is allowed to fill and is then scooped empty three times, the fourth inundation will be palatable and a continuing source. The same trunk can be used for up to four days, after which you can make another such reservoir. It's a good idea to keep the basin covered with something like a banana leaf to keep out insects and debris.

SALT DEFICIENCY

The loss of salt goes along with the loss of perspiration, and when you do more of the second you need more of the first. This is particularly noticeable when you are traveling in dry climates in which much of the sweating is not obvious. Otherwise, you may be able to get by using more salt on your food, although in the desert salt tablets are more convenient and reliable. Any drugstore can inexpensively procure them for you, but only experimentation can tell you how many you need.

Heat exhaustion goes hand in hand with salt deficiency, and if in low-humidity country such as the desert your muscles begin to ache unduly and your thinking wanders, try taking one or more tablets. Ordinary kitchen salt will do as well; however, the one-ounce tablets are not only more convenient, but you can get them with thirty percent dextrose which acts as an energy boost. Generally, you can get on a routine in ratio with your metabolism. Depending on your weight and amount of exertion, a half-dozen or more tablets a day may not be out of line.

CHAPTER 6

Your Appetite Will Be Like Never Before

No one in sufficiently good physical condition to venture into the backwoods in the beginning ever need starve. Other books describe the wild fruits and vegetables available to everyone.

In the evergreen forests that cover a large part of our wild places, for example, the inner bark—the part between the outer bark and the wood—of any of the pines or other conifers can be scraped or cut from the trunks of the living trees and eaten either raw or cooked like noodles. Brewing the live green needles, which are starchy and edible when young, into a strong dark tea with a Christmas tree flavor will both ward off and cure scurvy, which killed untold thousands in the old days. Beyond the timberline in the Far North, all vegetation with the exception of one mushroom is edible, although it is necessary first to soak the bitterness out of some of innumerable lichens to avoid digestive upset.

Some 300,000 plants, many of them variations of the same general type, grow in our world, and nearly half of these are edible. However, never take any chances. Some plants eaten by animals, such as the horse's poison ivy and the squirrel's deadly amanita mushroom, cannot be tolerated by humans. You'll do best either to take along a textbook or two on the subject or to familiarize yourself with the more common wild edibles in the area to which you are going before you take to the woods.

In fact, becoming familiar with a few more edible plants about your home, no matter where this may be, can become a pleasant and enthralling pastime, as well as a healthy way of pleasantly introducing free and fresh delicacies to family and guests. The knowledge thus acquired can even mean the difference—sometime, somewhere—between eating lavishly and starving.

On the other hand, it is important enough to repeat, "Never take any chances." If in an emergency it seems necessary, taste a very small amount of an abundant, favorable-looking plant. Then wait twenty-four hours. If all appears well, eat more of the plant and wait another day. If no ill effects appear, you may safely regard the plant as edible. However, short of a calamity, such as perhaps an overturned canoe, you are going to be well equipped with flour, baking powder, dried eggs and skimmed milk powder, margarine or canned butter, bacon, dried fruits, macaroni, lard, and the like.

Nearly everyone throws back to some degree to the characteristics of his caveman ancestors and, on occasion, finds satisfaction in eating for a time like a primitive being, especially if he can enliven his meals with delectable offbeat dishes.

MOOSE NOSE

"The great delicacies of the North American wilderness," Vilhjalmur Stefansson, most eminent of the recent terrestrial explorers, told me a few years ago, "are moose nose, beaver tail, buffalo hump, caribou brisket, and ling liver, all of them the delicious fat that it is now the fashion to condemn."

Like Dr. Stefansson, I've enjoyed all these. Especially when open flames are flickering, and there's the added relish of good companionship, it would be hard to pick five free edibles that are more delicious.

Moose nose is a favorite among Indians and many sourdoughs in the northwestern wilds of this continent where I've

enjoyed log-cabin living during much of the past three decades. The way you go at it with this biggest of all deer, prehistoric or otherwise, is to cut off the large upper jaw just below the eyes. Don't try to skin this. Instead, scald it in a pot of bubbling water, simmer about an hour, cool, and pluck. Then cook just short of boiling in fresh water, along with salt and pepper and if you like onions, until the white meat falls away from the nostrils and dark strips loosen from the bones and jowls. In the meantime, the pot hung over the hardwood coals of the campfire will be sending out tantalizing clouds of pure wilderness splendor, presaging a sweet, odorous feast.

This is fine to pick at hot. If you can keep occupied with other tidbits, though, let the juices and the meat jell together, then savor the whole in cold slices.

CARIBOU BRISKET

Caribou, North America's most abundant game animal, is unforgettable, especially when you can select mature animals in their prime. Clouds and cold September rain closed down on me one time in the northern British Columbia mountains after we'd dropped a fat trophy bull when it was at its sleekest and tastiest just before the rut. The mist was too thick for hunting, which made the fire in the cook tent all the cozier, for we were just out on a pack horse hunt.

Having plenty of leisure that particular day, we got things going by sautéing a cup each of chopped celery and chopped onion in 2 tablespoons of canned butter, along with the contents of a small can of mushrooms. This we seasoned with a teaspoon of salt, then mixed a cup of dry bread crumbs with it.

We spooned the lot over four thick slices of caribou brisket—enough, we reckoned, for two hungry hunters. These went into a flat pan and a 425° oven in my folding Sims stove. After the meat had browned for 10 minutes, we turned it to bronze for 10 minutes on the other side. By this time, the hardwood in the sheet-metal stove had fallen into coals which, with occasional replenishments, maintained a low, even heat for the next hour. We couldn't have waited any longer, anyway.

While we were eating, the nearby horse bells seemed to become louder and more distinct. When we shoved the whipping canvas flaps aside, it was to find a breeze scudding through the peaks and the air nearly clear. We glassed a couple of heavy-headed shapes on the cliffs opposite. Two days later we were broiling savory Stone-sheep steaks, one delicacy omitted by Dr. Stefansson that I'd surely include among the continent's greats.

MOUNTAIN SHEEP

The most coveted prize among North America's big game animals is the mountain sheep. The superlative meat is cooked like venison, although many don't want anything impinging upon the ambrosial natural flavor but salt, butter or margarine, and perhaps a little black pepper. When you're making stews, it's advisable to stick to the blander vegetables, such as potatoes, carrots, and parsnips, for this reason.

Wild mint *(Mentha),* though, is pleasing with large, rare roasts. We can make a sauce of this by heating ½ cup vinegar, ⅓ cup sugar, and ¼ teaspoon salt. Stir in finely chopped young mint leaves to taste, about ⅓ cup, and let the sauce cool an hour before serving. But even this wild mint sauce, we find, should be used sparingly with this king of the epicurean repasts.

BUFFALO HUMP

With buffalo now legal game around Canada's Great Slave Lake and occasionally in our forty-ninth state, and with surplus bison regularly being harvested in both countries, buffalo hump is again being savored by more and more North Americans.

When I can come by a substantial chunk, with its characteristic streaks of orangish fat, I like to salt it lightly, then
shove it into a moderately warm 350° oven or reflector baker,
with the fattest portion uppermost, to roast slowly, uncovered,
while basting itself to a turn. This is much too good, a lot of
us figure, to serve any other way but rare.

BEAVER TAIL

Dry oven heat or hanging in front of a small glowing fire will
cause the scaly dark skin of the beaver's flat tail to puff and lift
away in sections, exposing a fat, white, gelatinous meat. The
way I've come to enjoy this best is in a thick pea soup, good
enough to make an innocent think he is eating his way across
France.

Place two quarts of cold water, two cups of split peas, and a
small, skinned, cut-up beaver tail in a large kettle. Bring to a
boil and skim. Then add a large chopped onion, a cup of diced
celery, wild or otherwise, ½ cup diced carrots, ⅛ teaspoon
thyme if you happen to have any, and a bay leaf if that tree
grows thereabouts.

Simmer for two hours or until the meat separates from the
bones. Remove the beaver from the soup. Discard the bones and
the bay leaf.

Either press the vegetables through a sieve or puree them
the best way you can. Return the meat and vegetables, along
with the liquid, to the kettle. Season to taste with salt and
black pepper. Bring again to a simmer and ladle out piping hot.

LING LIVER

The greatest delicacy among the free foods, Stef always
avowed to me, is ling liver. Ling aren't the sportiest fish
within casting distance of our cabin, but these fresh-water
cod, which scientists call living fossils, certainly more than
hold their own against the arctic graylings and the rainbow
trout when it comes to eating.

The ling's tastiest parts are their large, fat, vitamin-replete livers. Generally, I ease on the frypan when coming up from the Peace River, melt a little margarine, and briefly sauté them— all the while hoping that no stranger will wander into sight until we've devoured them on the spot. There are times, I'm sure even my friend Stef would have agreed, when you can overdo the companionship bit.

SMALL GAME

The way snow was steaming at the fringes of my fire, while trees snapped and the ground boomed in the deepening cold, did nothing to detract from the best feed of small game I've ever eaten. Then, too, there was an aquamarine sky alive with the aurora borealis and the companionship of my Irish wolfhound pack dog, all conducive to hearty appetite.

Your hunger would really have been something, too, if you'd spent the better part of a British Columbia afternoon following fresh grizzly tracks. Spring had come late to the Peace River mountains that year, but day after day of melting chinook breezes had blown in. Frigid northeast winds suddenly undercut these in the frosty blueness of late afternoon. Snow began to granulate and crust beneath my feet. Finally, I saw where the big bear had paused for a backward look, then lifted his walk to a lope, and I turned back to where I had cached my small outfit.

Ordinarily, I'd have settled that night for beans, bacon, and bannock. But I had earlier crossed the trail of a friend, Joe Barkley, who was out beaver trapping, and he'd given me a plump, young hindquarter. I browned this on both sides in its own fat, sprinkled chopped onion over it while still forking it around, and salted and peppered it. Then I tipped in enough hot water from the boiling kettle to cover the bottom of the frypan, slid on a lid, and eased the whole thing in where enough birch coals were glowing apart to keep it simmering while I made camp.

Particles of heavying frost had started to drift down in the subzero stillness when, about an hour later, my fork slipped easily into the sputtering quarter. Helped along with gravy-dripping baking powder biscuits, and sluiced down with mug after mug of seething black tea, that meat was delicious.

Incidentally, this is one of the ways I cook beaver on a home stove, proving that some of the most delectable dishes in the world are of a pristine simplicity, while still boasting an elusive savor beyond the most elaborate continental concoctions.

Trees, ice, and ground were cannonading with cold when I finally dropped off to sleep. But what brought me awake, twisting in my down bag, was the drip of water. It was chinooking again. The remaining beaver proved moist and tasty in sandwiches that day and the next. By the time it was gone, I was sitting down to a feast of grizzly liver and not much else. But happily!

Fresh, plump meat is the single natural food that contains all the nutritional ingredients essential for mankind's good health. Neither anything else nor any particular portions need be eaten. Savory roasts, if that is what you prefer, will furnish you with all the nourishment needed to keep you robust even if you eat nothing else for a month, a year, or a decade.

One way to accomplish this in gourmet fashion during these days of high prices? By not passing up the small game that is freely available to many of us, often throughout the year, and which in numerous cases, as when there is a woodchuck shooter in the family, will only be wasted if not eaten.

Much small game is considerably more of a treat than deer, moose, caribou, and their ilk because of its fat. One tip, at any meal? Try to have enough of everything for seconds.

FRIED RABBIT

There is one point important enough to repeat for those who for one reason or another decide to keep going on an all-meat diet. This is that the game must have sufficient fat. One animal that doesn't is the rabbit. So-called rabbit starvation is well known in the North where I live. The salt-hungry snowshoe rabbits, which multiply and then decrease again in approximate six-year cycles, become so thick that once they dropped a shelter onto my unoccupied sleeping bag by gnawing the guy ropes. Try to live for even a week or ten days on an exclusive diet of the nearly fat-free rabbit and you'll starve to death, dying of nephritis. Yet, because it is so good when fat is added, the rabbit is North America's most hunted game.

Here's my favorite way of cooking it. Divide the rabbit or hare into serving pieces, disjointing whenever possible. Dip each portion in milk. Salt and pepper, then roll lightly in flour. Put ½ stick of margarine and 4 tablespoons cooking oil in a frypan over high heat and set in the pieces, any bony sides up. Lower the temperature at once and cook, uncovered, until the portions are brown on one side. Then turn, just once, and brown the other side. The meat will be crisp and done in a total of slightly more than half an hour. Spread it out on absorbent paper and keep warm while concocting the gravy.

For this, pour off all the fat except just enough to cover the bottom of the frypan, and save it for other eating uses. Stir in 2 tablespoons flour, ½ teaspoon salt, and ⅛ teaspoon black pepper, smoothing it into a paste. Using the milk into which you've dipped the meat, add enough additional milk to make a cupful. Pour this, then a cup of water, slowly into the pan, all the time stirring. Simmer over low heat for 12 minutes, adding more milk and water if the gravy becomes too thick. With everything served hot, this gravy has enough distinctness to transmute fried rabbit into an art form.

SAUTEED SQUIRREL

Once the prime target of buckskinned pioneers, the many squirrels that chatter across the continent still provide gourmet eating, particularly as these small trophies, like rabbits, have little if any gaminess.

The sweet, velvety, short-fibered meat is especially good sautéed. Just cut it into serving pieces. Forking these over frequently, brown them quickly with a liberal amount of margarine in a frypan. Then season to taste with salt and black pepper, lower the heat, and cook until tender.

Or if the game is a bit on the mature side, bronze the sections in a stick of margarine for half an hour or until nearly tender. Then cover with hard cider or such and simmer until this has been absorbed and evaporated. Finally, melt 2 tablespoons of margarine and sauté the portions until they are crisp. This is truly a sportsman's dish.

PORCUPINE STEW

"Many campers would pass up a porcupine, on which there is even a bounty in some places, and yet he is the purest of all vegetarians," Colonel Townsend Whelen told me when we were writing our book, *On Your Own in the Wilderness*. "My memory goes back to when Bones Andrews, one of the last of the old mountainmen of the breed of Jim Bridger, and I were compelled to spend several weeks in a region where there was no game. At the end of that time we had about the worst case of meat fever you can imagine. So we saddled up our little pack train and made tracks for higher altitudes and game country. On the way up I shot a porcupine. I skinned it, starting on the smooth underneath, and tied it to the back of my saddle.

"That night we made it into a stew. First, we cut it into small pieces and boiled these an hour. Then we added a handful of rice, some salt, a dozen small dumplings of biscuit dough, and covered all that to boil 20 minutes longer. This was tall country. With air pressures lessening with the altitude, the higher you climb, the longer you have to boil. We finished by adding a little flour to thicken the gravy and by stirring in a teaspoon of curry powder.

"Then the two of us sat down and finished the whole pot at one sitting. That pot held nine quarts and was full."

BY HOOK AND BY COOK

The way you cook your fish may be determined to some extent by their fatness. Plumper varieties, such as lake trout, salmon, and whitefish, are best for baking in a reflector baker or Dutch oven or for broiling over the cherry-red coals of a campfire. Their fat content helps them from becoming too dry. Leaner catches, such as pike, bass, perch, and arctic grayling, are preferable for poaching and for steaming because they remain firmer. They can also be satisfactorily baked and grilled if they are frequently basted or if topped with a sauce.

All fish are eminently suitable for frying. As far as that goes, any fish may be satisfactorily cooked by any of the basic methods if allowances are made for the fat content.

The main thing is not to overcook the catch. To keep fish moist and tender, and to bring out its delicate flavor, cook only until the flesh is no longer translucent. Once the fish is easily flaked with a stick or fork, it is done. The taste will be further enhanced if the fish is salted, inside and out, as much as an hour in advance of cooking.

Second thing to avoid? Never soak any fish before or after it is cleaned.

When you have a mess of small brook trout or such, let everyone roughly trim and peel his own green, hardwood, forked stick. Lay a slice of bacon on the wand and broil it over ruddy coals until translucent. Then place the opened and cleaned fish, skin down, atop the fork or stick and lay the bacon over it. Cook slowly over glowing embers. Repeat as long as fish and appetites hold out. There's rapture in such a meal.

GAME BIRDS

Are men the best cooks? The Hudson's Bay Company, drawing on over 300 years of North American experience, says so. In its cooking course aimed at the bachelor managers among its some 200 far-flung fur trading posts, the *Governor and Company of Adventurers of England Trading into Hudson's Bay* states unequivocally, "The best cooks in the world are men."

My wife Vena suspects that this statement may be inserted largely as a morale builder, because a few sentences further along the potential "world's best chef" is cautioned not to use his dishcloth to wipe off the stove. Yet the majority of good cooks in the Far North, certainly, are male. Some visiting sportsmen never do recover completely from the spectacle of hairy-armed sourdoughs lounging around a fur press and swapping recipes.

These old-timers go in mostly for plain cooking, although occasionally you'll meet a bannock-puncher with a flair for the exceptional. One of these was my friend, rotund Ted Boynton, famous for more than a quarter-century as one of the best trail cooks in the continental Northwest.

Whenever I see someone discarding some less favored waterfowl because they are "too fishy" or "too gamy" I remember how Ted Boynton used to handle birds of this sort. It's too bad, for several reasons, that more hunters don't know about it. Anyway, I guess one party figured they had Ted stopped the day they lugged in a brace of mud hen. One dude allowed as how he'd tried mud hen before. He said that if the part he got went over the fence last, someone must have given it a boost.

Maybe it was the odors sifting into the atmosphere from the direction of Ted Boynton's fire. Maybe it was just curiosity, for a mud hen, although kind to its family and all, is generally about as tender and tasty as a discarded moccasin. At any rate, there was no second call that evening after the first pan-banging-accompanied "Come and get it." There those fowl were, browned and bulging, looking as handsome as canvasback and smelling no less tempting than fat ptarmigan. Someone stuck his fork gingerly into a drumstick. Moist steaming meat fell invitingly away from the bone. Everyone dug in hungrily.

"Even a loon don't cook up too bad," Ted told us, and later proved, "if a yahoo don't try to gentle it aitch-for-leather. So don't throw mud hens or other such critters away, particularly in times like these. Skin and take out all fat. Then cram with onions. B'il real easy for 3 hours. Then start brand new with a crumb stuffing. Tuck a mess of sow belly or bacon strips where they'll do the most good. And roast nice and quiet like until a hungry man can't wait no longer."

GROUSE AND SUCH

The subtly flavored meat of one of the big, plump grouse is not far from the best you're going to sit down to in the game bird realm. The way I like them is cut into serving pieces, well rubbed with margarine or cooking oil, liberally salted, dusted with a few flakes of pepper, and then slowly broiled over hot coals. Start with the bony side down. Turn after about 10 minutes, again basting and seasoning. When a fork slips in easily and there's no gushing of red juices, the grouse is done.

You sometimes get a coatful of grouse or ptarmigan, though, in high windy country where there's no satisfactory hardwood for coals. One way around this is to use just the legs and breasts, saving the giblets and the rest for soup. Dredge the legs and breasts in salted and peppered flour. Now bring six slices of bacon slowly to sputter in a frypan. Remove the bacon to a hot dish when it is crisp. Quickly brown the birds on both sides in the hot fat. Salt and pepper them, then move to more moderate heat. Cover and cook 15 minutes, turning at about the halfway point.

Put the fowl on the hot dish with the bacon. Stir 2 tablespoons of flour into the fat and juice. Still stirring, add slowly 1½ cups milk. When this has thickened the way you like it, season it to taste. Let each banqueter spoon his share over fowl, bacon, and any vegetables. With one ridge after another lifting in front of the late northern sun as you eat, and a breeze starting to trumpet a cool blue note, this is grub you're never going to forget.

GRILLED VENISON STEAKS

This country came of age eating venison and wearing buckskin. We were weaned as a republic on deer meat, took our first venturesome steps in deer hide moccasins, and saw our initial light through buckskin—scraped, greased, and stretched over log cabin windows in place of glass. Today, because of care and wise game laws, deer are even thicker in parts of this country than during pioneer days.

With venison in particular—and this includes moose, caribou, elk, and their ilk—where the toughening and drying effects of overcooking should be avoided if at all possible, the steaks should not be laid too near a too ardent fire. This distance should be increased, not decreased, with thicker steaks.

The thicker the steak, the longer the meat must be cooked if the heat is to penetrate to its center. If too close for too long, the exterior will overcook and toughen.

Good, tender venison will be at its sizzling best when least disguised by seasoning. All that is wanted is a scattering of salt, and maybe a melting slab of butter or margarine just before eating.

Grill the steaks just long enough to satisfy the eater's taste. Overcooking ruins most big game meat, with the exception of bear, because of its general lack of the layers of fat common to comparable domestic cuts. Such wild meat dries out in heat, and the fibers quickly harden and toughen.

If your venison is from an older animal, treat it before cooking with a non-seasoned meat tenderizer. For the best results with game, use ¾ teaspoon per pound of meat and let it stand 20 to 30 minutes at room temperature for each half inch of thickness. Frozen game must, of course, be thawed first.

Pricking or gashing the steak is the most practical way to test doneness. The welling out of red juice indicates the meat is rare. If the fluid is pink, the meat is medium rare. Colorless? It's overdone unless that's the way it is preferred.

BEAR

You'll probably have to try it to believe it, but properly cooked bear is comparable to the best prime beef. However, bear steaks are never satisfactory. The meat is essentially stringy, and because of a possibility of trichinosis, it must be cooked too long to make a good steak. Unlike other game meats, bear should always be well done. The generally inherent fat will prevent it from drying out, so the extra heat makes it all the more savory. Except in the spring, trim off all but about half an inch of fat. In the springtime, when the bear is generally lean from its long sleep (which incidentally is not hibernation), lard liberally with beef fat, the thing also to use with venison. When the bear is lean, baste all exposed portions about every 10 minutes after the first hour.

Place the meat with the bone, if any, toward the bottom on a rack in an open pan. Don't flour or sear. Moderately slow heat, about 325°, will give the best results. Bear varies considerably in texture, so the only rule that can be given is to roast it until tender. When a large sharp fork can be easily inserted, then withdrawn without binding, the meat will be ready. Because of the absolutely delightful aroma given off by roasting bear, so will everyone else. You can almost hear the creaking wheels of covered wagon trains when you eat grub like this.

BEAR CRACKLINGS

You'll be passing up some of the best shortening available anywhere if you don't render all bear fat in moderate heat in open oven or reflector baker pans, then strain the liquid into jars. That from the black bear will harden into a clear white lard, while that from the grizzly will remain a more easily measured oil. The remaining cracklings are tasty and pleasingly crisp to nibble.

COOKING UTENSILS

Except for a large boiling utensil, which will be practically a necessity if you plan to live to any reasonable degree off the country, you can get along without much of a cooking outfit. Handiest of all in the culinary department is one of the small nested sets that are available at sporting goods stores and through some of the large catalog-issuing firms like Abercrombie & Fitch, Madison Avenue at 45th Street, New York 10017. By all means get the best obtainable. Even this will be far more functional if the cups, and preferably the plates as well, are made of stainless steel rather than of the more fragile, all too fast-heating aluminum. A steel frypan with a folding handle is a wise choice as well. Get stainless steel tools.

TREELESS MAPLE SYRUP

The sugar maple grows only in North America. Like all green trees, it mysteriously changes water and carbon dioxide into sugar. So exceptional is the maple syrup's capacity for storing the sweet that this talent is a double boon. In autumn, it produces some of the loveliest hues of the North American forest; in spring, the amber succulence of maple syrup.

The only trouble many wilderness cooks have is that these latter activities are largely confined to such Eastern regions as the St. Lawrence Valley, New Brunswick and Nova Scotia, and such New England states as New Hampshire and Vermont. But there's an ingenious way around.

You'll need: 6 medium potatoes, 2 cups water, 1 cup apiece of brown and white sugars. Peel the medium-size potatoes. Boil uncovered with 2 cups water for use any way you want, then remove once 1 cup of fluid remains. Stirring the liquid until it again reaches the boiling point, slowly add the sugar. Once this has completely dissolved, set the pan off the heat to cool slowly.

"Ghastly concoction," Dudley Shaw, the old mountainman who gave me the formula, nodded agreeably when I sampled the elixir at this primary stage. "Like home brew, it has to be aged in a dark place. After a couple of days in a corked bottle it'll be noble."

See if that first spoonful you doubtfully try doesn't seem to justify your worst suspicions, too. But bottle the syrup and tuck it away for several days to age. Try it again at the end of that time and see if you, also, aren't pleasantly amazed.

DUTCH OVENS, REFLECTOR BAKERS, ETC.

If you're traveling in such a way that space and weight are of little consequence, as with a pack string or canoe with few portages, by all means bring a Dutch oven, a folding stove and oven, and a folding reflector baker. There is no room to consider these in the desired detail in this book. Carry my small, lightweight, all-inclusive *Wilderness Cookery*. But one thing we can cover is a small oven thermometer which costs only a few cents, occupies very little room, and takes much of the initial guesswork out of baking with outdoor fires. The following table will then apply; all temperatures in this book are the commonly used Fahrenheit, by which at sea level fresh water freezes at 32° and boils at 212°.

Slow oven	250° to 325°
Moderate oven	325° to 400°
Hot oven	400° to 450°
Very hot oven	450° to 550°

If you're starting out with no such thermometer, you will be able to get a fairly accurate idea of the temperature by using the following test. With experience, of course, you'll be able to make the same approximations by holding the bare hand in the heat. In the meantime, sprinkle some white flour in a pan and place this in the heated oven or reflector baker. If you're

Cooking and Baking Equipment

Top: Reflector Baker. *Middle:* Reflector baker used with folding stove.
Bottom: Dutch oven.

short on flour, a piece of white tissue paper can be used instead. All testing times but the last are five minutes.

Turns light tan	Slow oven
Turns medium golden tan	Moderate oven
Turns deep dark brown	Hot oven
Turns deep dark brown in 3 minutes	Very hot oven

LIGHTWEIGHT RATIONS

For the long pull, you'll find that fat, in calories the most concentrated of food, is the hardest to come by when you're living to any extent off the country. Butter, margarine, bacon drippings, and lard for example boast more than double the calories, ounce for ounce, of such a staple as sugar and nearly three times as much as honey. For limited rations on wilderness stints of undetermined duration you may decide, therefore, to take along a preponderance of edible fats with the idea of partly completing your diet from natural sources.

For a shorter haul, you may care to include some of the tasty, compact, and nutritious rations now specially manufactured for campers as a whole, expeditions, mountain climbers, backwoodsmen, and others who want to get back of beyond under their own steam.

While in the wilderness writing this book, I've had the enjoyment of testing under go-light conditions the preassembled meals and other dehydrated foods designed for trail and camp by Chuck Wagon Foods, Micro Drive, Woburn, Massachusetts 01801. I find them sustaining and pleasant, as well as light, compactly put together, and efficient. Richard A. Smith now heads this concern. Dick is alert to backwoods needs, with a long and comprehensive list of dehydrated fruits, vegetables, meats, and such.

Bill White, Stow-A-Way Sports Industries, Cushing Highway, Cohasset, Massachusetts 02025, also has a fine and discriminating line of foods, as well as other needs for the backwoodsman.

TIPS ON PACKING AND STORING FOOD

Dry foods such as flour, cereal, beans, salt, spices, and other essentials such as dehydrated eggs and milk can be packed in small moistureproof sacks which are available in a variety of types and sizes from most camp outfitters. You can make such packets yourself, too. Each should be very plainly and indestructably labeled. Repackage dry food such as spices, fruit powders, and the like whenever this can be done advantageously, cutting out and including any special directions. Unless you've ample room, unnecessarily bulky foods such as corn flakes should be compressed into as small a space as practical.

Dried meats may be wrapped in aluminum foil or clinging harmless plastic. Lard, margarine, and the like travel well in tightly closed aluminum containers. Plastic flasks and bottles made for carrying most liquids are safer and lighter than glass for syrup, oil, and such, but definitely not for most extracts.

CHEESE

Cheese, which goes very well with jam in sandwiches, is one of the most versatile, nourishing, and delectable of camp foods. It may be relished in its natural state or added to everything from soups and salads to sauces to make all sorts of delicious combinations. A sharp, aged cheddar keeps well, as do edam and gouda. Provalone is probably the best choice in high temperatures.

If heat makes your cheese rubbery, a solution is to wrap it well and revive it in a cool stream. If you're going to spend a month or more away from civilization, sew one-week portions snugly in cheesecloth and immerse them in melted wax. You can harmlessly keep mold off cheese to a large extent by wiping the cheese in a clean cloth soaked either in baking soda solution or in vinegar. The same thing goes for sliced bacon.

DRY MILK

Powdered milk is especially handy in cold weather if only because the quality of evaporated milk is impaired by freezing which, for that matter, can cause it to spoil entirely by bursting the can. Besides, evaporated milk is still three-fourths water. Condensed milk is one-fourth water and nearly one-half sugar. Depending on the product, one pound of whole milk makes one gallon of liquid whole milk.

Dried skim milk has all the nourishment of fresh skim milk. It has the calcium, phosphorus, iron and other minerals, the B vitamins, natural sugar, and the protein that make liquid skim milk such an important food. Powdered whole milk has all these, plus the fat and vitamin A found in the cream of whole milk. Adding two teaspoons of butter or margarine to a cup of reconstituted skim milk will make this equal in food value to a cup of whole milk.

POWDERED EGGS

An egg is 11 percent waste unless you are going to bake the shells and then pulverize them, as some do to increase the calcium content of their pack and sled dogs' food. Of the remaining white and yolk, 74 percent is water. Yet whole dried egg has virtually the same food value, includes not a bit of waste, and has only a minute proportion of water.

The flavor of egg powder cooked by itself is not like that of fresh eggs. Most of us in the contiguous United States are accustomed to the latter. Our natural taste reaction, therefore, is that the former is inferior. With different eating habits, as many have witnessed in Europe, this taste prejudice also works the other way around.

In any event, scrambled eggs made from the powder come to taste mighty good back of beyond. If you haven't prepared these before, dissolve powdered eggs and milk in luke-warm water to make the proportions of those fresh products you would ordinarily use. Add salt, pepper, and any other seasoning, together with a chunk of butter or margarine. A little flour may be stirred in for thickening. Scrambling all this with ham or bacon gives the dish added flavor.

SOURDOUGH BREAD

Sourdough bread is particularly designed to solve the problems of the ofttimes unskilled wilderness cook. Considerable folklore has sprung up around this pioneer staple which, early proving its ability to rise under just about any condition short of freezing, gave veteran northerners their title of "sourdoughs". You hear tales of sourdough that has been kept going ever since Alaskan and Klondike gold rush days near the turn of the century. Many such accounts are completely true.

For real sourdough bread on the trail, you can get a dollar packet of Bradford Angier Sourdough Starter, plus a pamphlet of instructions and recipes, from your store. These are put out by Chuck Wagon Foods, Micro Drive, Woburn, Massachusetts 01801, or write to me at Hudson Hope, British Columbia, Canada, including fifty cents for postage and handling, and I'll rush one to you first class. Once you have this starter, you're all set for life. You'll never have to buy yeast again. You'll have commenced growing your own yeast.

If you prefer, try your hand at making your own primitive sourdough starter by putting a cup apiece of plain flour and cold water in a scalded jar, covering it loosely, and placing it in a warm place to sour. If the initial results are unsatisfactory—and it all depends on what wild yeasts you capture from the air—throw out what you have, rescald the jar, and try again with a new mixture of flour and water. When ready, the starter should be bubbling, increasing in size, and smelling pleasantly yeasty.

Take your starter. Add equal amounts of flour and lukewarm water to make about 3 cups of sponge. Mix well. Let stand, covered, in a warm spot overnight or at least for a minimum of 6 to 8 hours, whereupon it should be bubbling and emitting agreeable, yeasty odor.

Take out a cup of this sponge and place in a well-washed and scalded glass or pottery container. Keep in a cool spot. This is your next starter. No matter what the recipe, at this stage always keep out a cup of the basic sourdough.

Mix 5 cups of flour with 2 tablespoons of sugar and a teaspoon of salt. Make a depression in the center of these dry ingredients. Pour the remaining 2 cups of sponge in this. Then mix ½ cup of milk, a tablespoon of melted shortening, and a cup of hot water. When the liquid is lukewarm (blood temperature), add the rest of the ingredients and mix well. Add more flour if needed to make a workable dough. On a lightly floured board knead for 3 or 4 minutes if you want a finer textured bread.

Put the dough in a large greased and covered bowl. Let rise until doubled in size, then punch it down. Knead it another 2 to 4 minutes, divide into loaves, and let rise again. Cook at about 400°, in a moderate oven or reflector baker, for an hour.

Baking should redouble the size of the loaves. When the bread seems done, perhaps crisply brown, test by jabbing in a straw. If the bread is ready, the straw will come out dry and clean. With a little more experience, listen for the hollow sound the finished loaves will give when thumped on top. Remove from the oven, turn out on a rack or towel and, if you like, butter the tops.

Sourdough bread is substantial in comparison with the usual air-filled bakery loaf. It keeps moist for a satisfyingly long time. When the bread is made according to the preceding suggestions, the flavor is unusually excellent, and becomes especially nutty when slices are toasted. If your family likes real tasty crust, bake the bread in slim loaves to capitalize on this outstanding characteristic.

BANNOCK

Bannock is the famous frying pan bread of the open places. The basic recipe for one hungry backwoodsman who's going to eat it with something else is: 1 cup flour, 1 teaspoon fresh double-action baking powder, and ½ teaspoon salt. Mix these dry, taking all the time you require to accomplish this thoroughly. Have the hands floured and everything ready to go before you add liquid, for then you'll have set free the carbon dioxide gas necessary for raising the breadstuff. If you are going to use the traditional frypan, make sure it is warm and greased and that you have a suitable cooking fire.

Working rapidly from now on, stir in enough cold water (the colder the better) to make a firm dough. Shape this, with as little handling as possible, into a cake about one inch thick. If you particularly like crust, leave a doughnutlike hole in the center. In any event, dust the loaf lightly with flour so that it will handle easily. Lay the bannock in the warm, greased frypan. Hold it over the heat until a bottom crust forms, rotating the pan a little so the loaf will shift and not become stuck.

Once the dough has hardened enough to hold together, you can turn the bannock over. This, if you've practiced a bit and have the confidence to flip strongly enough, can be easily accomplished with a slight swing of the arm and snap of the wrist. Or you can use a flour-sprinkled plate or spatula, supporting the loaf long enough to reverse the frypan again and slide the uncooked portion of loaf to the bottom of the pan and return pan and bannock to the heat.

With a campfire, however, it is often easier at this stage just to prop the frypan at a steep angle so that the bannock will get direct heat on top. When crust has formed all around, you may if you wish turn the bannock over and around a few times while it is cooking to an appetizing brown.

When is the bannock done? After you've been cooking them a while, you will be able to tap one and gauge doneness by the hollowness of the sound. Meanwhile, test by shoving in a straw or sliver. If any dough adheres, the loaf needs more heat. Cooking can be accomplished in about 15 minutes. If you have other duties around camp, twice that time a bit further from the heat will allow the bannock to cook more evenly.

Bannock, in any event, never tastes better than when devoured piping hot around a campfire. It should then be broken apart, never cut. A cold bannock sliced in half, however, and made into a man-size sandwich with plenty of meat or other filler is the best lunch ever.

THE CALORIE STORY

You can, if weight and space are at an extreme premium, use a calorie chart as a basis for figuring how to go about packing the most nourishment with the least trouble. Briefly, you're burning up a certain amount of energy every second. Energy not supplied directly by a sufficiency of food is taken from the body's carbohydrates, fats, and proteins.

Even when you're sleeping relaxed in the most comfortable of eiderdowns, your system is consuming heat units, or calories, at the rate of approximately 10 calories a day per pound of body weight. In other words, if you weigh 160 pounds, the least number of calories you'll use each day is 1,600. These basic requirements diminish but slightly, as a matter of fact, even when an individual is starving.

The more you move around and the more energy you expend in keeping warm, the more calories you use. Even lying in your sleeping bag and reading will increase your basic caloric needs about 25 percent. The city man who gets very little exercise consumes on the average 50 percent above his minimum requirements. To maintain his weight, therefore, such a 160-pound individual requires about 2,400 calories daily.

It is reasonable, both from these scientific facts and from personal experience, to generalize that a healthy and fit man enjoying a robust outdoor life can require 20 calories of food a day per pound of body weight—and perhaps more, depending on his activity and the climate. Cold weather, for example, compels the system to put out more and more heat to keep itself warm. The same 160-pound city man adventuring in the North Woods can very easily ingest 3,200 or 4,000 calories, and more, a day and still firm up lean and hard.

PROVISIONING FOR THE BACKWOODS

When appetites are sharpened by the type of vigorous, healthy, sound, flourishing, wholesome, hale, and robust outdoor living for which men and women were bred, meals afield can be just as nourishing and tasty as those in town—and maybe more so—when you take foods that keep well, cook readily, and are easy to carry, and when you live to a reasonable and pleasurable extent off the country. There is no sound reason for suggesting any particular grub lists or daily menus, for what suits one will not always satisfy another. You'll do best to take what you personally like and what you'll find easiest to prepare.

Experimentation is the best way to learn how much of each item you'll need to round out a satisfactory meal. If you want oatmeal porridge each morning, for instance, find out just how many rolled oats are required to make the breakfast you will likely find sufficient in the field. Multiply by the days you'll be outdoors. Just as a suggestion, unless there is some reason against it take along at least twice the amount of sugar and sweets you'd use at home, for your desire for them will be out of all proportion to that in the asphalt jungles.

Here is a yardstick you may find valuable. Generally speaking, the total weight of reasonably water-free foods you will want to eat should not be less than 2¼ pounds per man per day. This does not include the fresh fruits and vegetables you'll likely find for the taking. For the purposes of figuring, the following chart may be used for more or less scientifically planning a light, compact grubstake made up largely of high-energy rations.

Cal.	One-Pound Portion	Outfitting Data
2709	Almonds, shelled, dried	1 cup shelled = 5⅓ oz.
1680	Apples, dried	1 lb. dried = 8 lbs. fresh
1634	Apricots, dried	1 lb. dry = 5½ lbs. fresh
1047	Bacon, back	3 slices, 2½″ diam. × ¼″ = 3½ oz.
2855	Bacon, side	1 lb. = 20 to 24 slices; 2½ to 3 slices = 2 oz.
1219	Banana, dried	3½ oz. dried = about 1 lb. fresh
1536	Barley, brown, whole	2 tbsp. dry = 1 oz.
1525	Beans, dried, kidney	1 lb. = 2⅔ cups 1 lb. = 7 cups cooked
1512	Beans, Lima	1 lb. = 2⅓ cups 1 lb. = 6½ cups cooked
1535	Beans, navy	1 lb. = 2⅓ cups 1 lb. = 6 cups cooked

Cal.	One-Pound Portion	Outfitting Data
922	Beef, dried or chipped	2 thin slices = 1 oz.
1044	Bologna	1 slice, 4½" diam. × ⅛" = 1 oz.
3248	Butter	1 lb. = 2 cups
1587	Cabbage, dehydrated	1 lb. serves 50
		1 serving = ⅓ oz.
1641	Carrots, dehydrated	1 lb. serves 25
		1 serving raw = 4 oz. cooked
2619	Cashews	4 to 5 nuts = ½ oz.
1804	Cheese, cheddar	1 lb. cheese grated = 4 cups
1676	Cheese, cheddar processed	1 lb. cheese grated = 4 cups
1679	Cheese, Swiss	1 slice, 4½" ×3½" × ⅛" = 1 oz.
905	Chicken, canned, boned	½ cup = 3½ oz.
2273	Chocolate, bitter	1 lb. melted = 2 cups
2282	Chocolate, milk, plain	1 lb. melted = 2 cups
2413	Chocolate, milk, with almonds	1 lb. melted = 2 cups
2403	Chocolate, bittersweet	1 lb. melted = 2 cups
2136	Chocolate, sweetened, plain	1 lb. melted = 2 cups
1329	Cocoa, dry	1 lb. = 4 cups
1316	Coffee, roasted	1 lb. = 5½ cups finely ground, makes 50 cups. Contains, in solid state, 1316 calories.
1649	Corn meal, yellow	3 cups = 1 lb.
4013	Corn oil	1 lb. = 2 cups
1642	Cornstarch	1 lb. = 3½ cups (stirred)
4013	Cotton seed oil	1 lb. = 2 cups
1287	Dates, dried, pitted	1 lb. pitted & cut = 2½ cups
2688	Egg, dried, whole	¼ cup powder & 1½ cups water = 1 doz. fresh eggs
1530	Farina, dark	3 tbsp. dry = 1 oz. = ¾ cup cooked
1677	Farina, light	1 lb. = approximately 2⅔ cups dry
1223	Figs, dried	3 cups (44 figs) = 1 lb.
2838	Filberts, shelled	1 cup = 4¾ oz.
1643	Flour, buckwheat, light	1 cup = 4¼ oz.
1574	Flour, dark	1 cup = 4¼ oz.
1659	Flour, rye, light	1 lb. = about 4½ cups
		1 lb. sifted = 5⅔ cups
1442	Flour, rye, dark	1 lb. = about 4½ cups
		1 lb. sifted = 5⅔ cups
1632	Flour, wheat, all-purpose	4 cups = 1 lb. sifted
1632	Flour, wheat, cake	4¾ cups = 1 lb. sifted
1632	Flour, wheat, pastry	4¾ cups = 1 lb. sifted
1510	Flour, whole wheat	3¾ cups = 1 lb. stirred
1739	Gelatin, dessert powder	2½ cups = 1 lb.
		1 oz. pkg. = 4 to 6 servings

Cal.	One-Pound Portion	Outfitting Data
1643	Hominy, grits	3 cups = 1 lb. 3 tbsp. raw = ⅔ cup cooked
1400	Honey	1⅓ cups = 1 lb.
1262	Jam, assorted	3 level tbsp. = 2 oz.
4091	Lard	2 cups = 1 lb. 2 tbsp. = 1 oz.
1530	Lentils, dry	2⅓ cups = 1 lb. 2½ tbsp. dry = 1 oz. = ½ cup cooked
1723	Macaroni	1 lb. 1″ pieces = 4 cups
2231	Milk, powdered, whole	1 lb. = 3½ cups 4 tbsp. level & 1 cup water = 1 cup fresh milk
1642	Milk, powdered, skim	⅓ cup & ¾ cup water = 1 cup fresh skim milk 3.2 oz. = 1 qt.
1142	Molasses	1 cup = 11 oz.
1728	Noodles, containing egg	1″ pieces = 6 cups to 1 lb. 1 lb. = 11 cups cooked
1794	Oats, meal or rolled	1 lb. = 5⅔ cups ⅓ cup = 1 cup porridge
3266	Oleomargarine	1 tbsp. = ½ oz.
4013	Olive oil	1 lb. = 2 cups
1634	Peaches, dried	1 lb. dried = 5½ lbs. fresh
2613	Peanut butter	1 lb. = 2 cups
1219	Pears, dried	1 lb. dried = 5½ lbs. fresh
1540	Peas, dried, green	2 tbsp. dry = 1 oz. =⅓ cup cooked
1562	Peas, split	2¼ cups = 1 lb.
3159	Pecans, shelled	1 lb. in shell = ⅓ lb. meats
3410	Pork, salt, fat, with rind	2 slices 4″ × 2″ × ⅜″ = 3½ oz.
1620	Potatoes, dehydrated	1 serving = 1 oz. dry = 4 oz. reconstituted
1725	Prunes, dried, pitted	1 lb. cooked with 2 qts. water = 2½ qts.
1217	Raisins, dried, seeded	3¼ cups = 1 lb.
	Raisins, dried, seedless	2¾ cups whole = 1 lb.
1648	Rice, brown	2 tbsp. dry = 1 oz. = ½ cup cooked
1629	Rice, white	1 lb. = 2⅛ cups = 7 cups when cooked
1682	Rice, wild	1 lb. = 3 cups 1 oz. = 3 tbsp. = 1 serving
1531	Sardines in oil	15 sardines, 3″ long = 5 oz.

Cal.	One-Pound Portion	Outfitting Data
4010	Shortening, vegetable, Crisco, Spry, etc.	1 lb. = 2¼ cups
3437	Suet	1 lb. ground suet = 3½ cups
1676	Sugar, brown	2 cups (firmly packed) = 1 lb.
1747	Sugar, granulated, white	1 lb. = 2¼ cups
1747	Sugar, icing	1 lb. = 3½ cups
1747	Sugar, loaf	100 flat tablets = 1 lb.
1299	Syrups, corn	1⅓ cups = 1 lb.
1123	Syrups, maple	1½ cups = 1 lb.
1633	Tapioca, dry, pearl	2¾ cups raw = 7½ cups cooked
	Tea	1 lb. = 6 cups dry = 200 to 300 cups
2969	Walnuts, shelled	1 lb. in shell = ⅓ cup meats
		1 lb. halves = 4½ cups
1639	Wheat, germ	1 tbsp. = ¹⁄₆ oz.
1544	Whole wheat, dry	⅓ cup dry = 1 oz. = ¾ cup cooked

The nutrient values, based on official researches of two governments with standard American and Canadian foods, will

vary somewhat in different localities. Dehydrated products will naturally differ to an even broader extent, depending not only on the original raw products but also on processing methods. Slight seasonal variations in food content have been ignored, being unimportant to the aspects here considered.

HUDSON'S BAY COMPANY PLUM PUDDING

If you're going to be hunting in the bush with a friend or two on the American or Canadian Thanksgiving and want to have something a little special for that occasion, you may be interested in going prepared to make one of the aromatic Hudson's Bay Company puddings which—traditionally varying in accordance with what ingredients are at hand—have crowned many a holiday feast in the silent places since the Company was founded 2 May 1670.

The following components can be mixed at home and sealed in a plastic container:

    4 cups sifted flour
    4 teaspoons double-action baking powder
    ½ teaspoon cinnamon
    ½ teaspoon nutmeg
    1 cup brown sugar
    ½ cup white sugar
    ¼ cup finely chopped glacéed fruit mix
    2 cups seedless raisins
    1 cup currants
    4 tablespoons dehydrated whole egg
    6 tablespoons dehydrated whole milk
    ¼ teaspoon powdered lemon juice

When the memorable day arrives, shake and stir all these ingredients together, along with 2 cups of finely minced suet. This can be either beef suet brought for the occasion or animal suet obtained on the spot. Add 2 cups water to make a cake batter. You will also have packed along a heavy cotton bag, and this you will have just wrung out in hot water and sprinkled inside with flour. Pour the batter into this. Tie the top tightly, leaving plenty of room for expansion.

Place immediately in a pot filled with sufficient boiling water to cover. Keep it boiling for three hours, turning the bag upside down when the pudding starts to harden so that all the fruit will not settle to the bottom. As the cooking continues, shift the bag occasionally so it will not scorch against the sides of the receptacle. At the end, dip this cloth container briefly in cold water and carefully remove the fabric so as not to break or crumble the pudding.

Serve this plum pudding hot with an appropriate sauce. Butter and sugar flavored with spice, such as nutmeg, an extract, or lemon powder, will suffice. So will the thick juice from boiled dehydrated fruit.

Every time I enjoy one of these in the bush I think of Voltaire acidly describing the North two centuries ago as "A patch of snow inhabited by barbarians, bear, and beaver." He should have seen the top of the continent when it's in a holiday mood.

SNOW ICE CREAM

One of the most enjoyable wilderness treats is devouring ice cream made by the simple practice of pouring a can of undiluted evaporated milk into a large pan or bowl, adding sugar and some flavor, and then stirring in loads of light, fresh snow until both texture and taste are pleasing. We've dined at gourmet establishments around the world, and we know of no more delectable dessert anywhere.

CHAPTER 7

Always Knowing Where You Are

One lost man I found in the New England woods, when I was still pretty much of a tenderfoot myself, had started running when he first realized he didn't know his whereabouts and hadn't stopped until he fell, exhausted, breaking a leg. Another for whom I joined the search in arid mountains just west of the soaring Grand Tetons years later had donned light moccasins to go down to the creek for water, missed camp on his way back with brimming pail, and had walked what turned out to be forty-two miles in a nearly straight line before being located, dehydrated and dead, coiled in a small cave, his feet actually worn through to the bones.

I've talked to other individuals who were found safe after being mislaid for one or two days, and they said it is the emptiest, bleakest, loneliest feeling in the world. Here's how to make sure its terrors never overtake you.

FREEDOM IN THE WILDS

You'll never feel utterly free in the wilderness until you're able to tell, anywhere at any time, almost exactly where you are. Far from being complicated, the procedure necessary for this is positive and permanent, an ever-intriguing problem of angles and distances. Even a youngster can learn it—often better than the typical native who is proceeding by knowledge of his territory and not by any instinct, which science has proved does not exist in man—from the simple details considered in this chapter.

The principal part of the procedure started about five thousand years ago when some Mongol, probably, found that if a longish chunk of a certain rock—magnetic, although he didn't know what this meant—was laid on a piece of wood large enough to keep it floating on still water, it would finally come to rest with one end pointing almost exactly along the shadow cast by the sun at midday. Or perhaps he even hung this length of magnetic rock on a thong, as Kubla Khan did years later.

THE NORTH STAR AND THE SOUTHERN CROSS

From this discovery, in any event, evolved the compass, now usually a light, slim length of magnetized steel so balanced that it will pivot freely. Previously, man had traveled by the sun or, more accurately, by the night stars. Primitive man finally understood that this early compass, for that is what he now had, pointed nearly precisely toward a certain star that we now know as Polaris or the North Star.

He learned that in the Northern Hemisphere this star, not as bright as many but having the peculiar characteristic of staying almost stationary in the heavens, could be recognized on clear nights by what we now call the Big Dipper (also known as the Big Bear). An imaginary line joining from bottom to top the two stars forming the outer side of the bowl, if extended some five times its length, will end near the North Star. This guiding star, so important to early mariners, is about the same brightness as the two pointers, and there are no bright stars in between. The pointers are about five degrees apart. And so it came about that the north end of these first crude compasses was important. If enterprising civilization had started and continued more assertively in the southern half of the world, it would have been the wavering sunward end of the early magnetic ores that would have become the more important, and the arrows and importantly marked ends of today's compasses would point south instead of north.

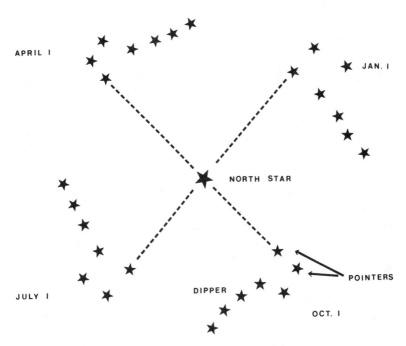

North Star and Big Dipper, Showing Pointers

When one travels south, the same sort of celestial navigation comes into being. There, as primitive man finally observed, what we now know as the Southern Cross is the most distinctive constellation in the Southern Hemisphere, coming into view shortly before the Big Dipper drops below the horizon behind us as we journey southward. An imaginary line carried through the longer axis of the Southern Cross points toward the South Pole. A pair of the four stars of the Southern Cross, also called the Crux, are among the most vivid in the night skies. These two are on the southern and eastern arms. The former, at the foot of the Cross, is known as Alpis Crusis and, when viewed through a telescope, turns out to be a magnificent double star. Those on the northern and western arms, while bright, are smaller.

Although the Southern Cross is the most celebrated of the constellations of the far south, it looks more like a kite than a cross and, so, is a disappointment to many world travelers when they view it for the first time. However, the fact that it lies nearer the South Pole than any other well-defined constellation gives it an importance, despite its smallness, comparable to that of the Big Dipper in the Northern Hemisphere. There is no star above the South Pole to correspond with our North Star. As a matter of fact, where such a star would gleam there exists a region which to the naked eye seems void of stars. This pear-shaped hole in the midst of an otherwise brilliant section of the Milky Way, like an island in its stream, is so dark that early sailors called it the Coal Sack, a name so apt that it has remained.

Also known as the True Cross, the Southern Cross should not be confused with the False Cross which has five stars, including the one in its center. The drawing shows the Southern Cross and, to its west, the False Cross. You may care to hold the book over your head for realism. Then note the two very bright stars just to the east of the Southern Cross. With them and the latter constellation as guides, you will be able to locate the point within the Coal Sack which is precisely over the South Pole.

First, extend an imaginary line along the long axis of the Southern Cross to the south. Then join the two bright stars to the east of the Southern Cross with another imaginary line. Bisect this latter line with one at right angles. The intersection of this latter line with the line through the Southern Cross is above the approximate position of the South Pole.

OTHER STARS IN THE NORTH

You can check the North Star by the fact that Polaris is the bright star at the free end of the handle of the far dimmer Little Dipper, which the Ancients called Ursa Minor, or Little Bear. This arrangement of stars, not as easily found as the Big Dipper and easily missed when the stars are obscured by even scant cloud cover or the brilliance of moonlight or the northern lights, pours its imaginary contents into the Big Dipper and vice versa.

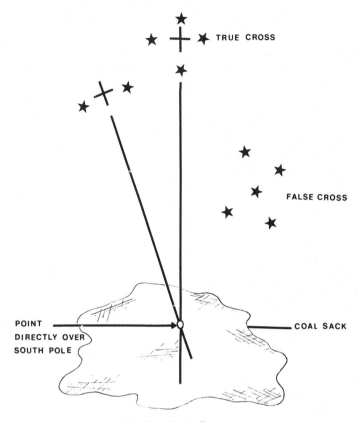

The Southern Cross

Too, the constellation known as Cassiopeia—the large W or M in the northern heavens, its shape depending on the time when it is seen—is always the same angle away from Polaris, as shown by the drawings. In the event that the Big Dipper is obscured and you want to know exactly where you are, it may be a sound procedure to memorize this relationship.

DEVELOPMENT OF THE MODERN COMPASS

Crude magnetic-ore compasses finally evolved into magnetized compass needles which the Chinese used nearly 1,000

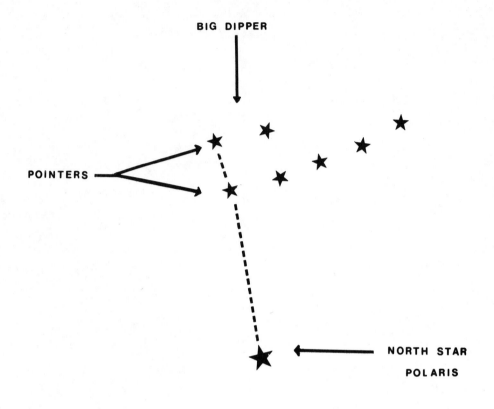

BIG DIPPER

POINTERS

NORTH STAR
POLARIS

CASSIOPEIA

Relation of Big Dipper and Cassiopeia to North Star

years ago, the Arabs about 100 years later, and the seafaring Vikings about a quarter-century further along. These earliest needles swung freely on a pivot in air-filled containers. The trouble with this was that, especially when referred to at sea and during the course of travel by animals, the wavering needle pointed only in a general direction.

This was eventually overcome by various methods, such as the device still used of bringing the needle to a swifter halt in the induction-dampened compass in which a copper-lined container, covered by a translucent surface, induces electrical currents that bring the needle to a faster stop. The most effective method up to the present time is to fill the housing, now often plastic, with a non-freezing liquid such as alcohol which retards the oscillations without interfering with accuracy.

READING A COMPASS

Many of today's compass faces are divided into the 360 degrees of every circle, each one of which may be regarded as a possible path to follow. For backwoods use, it is easier to consult one of the sixteen major compass directions. These directions are shown on the face of a modern marine compass, illustrated later in this chapter.

If you face north, for example, and raise your arms, south is at your back, west at your left and east at your right. This is too rough a definition for backwoods practice, so you break each of the four cardinal points into half, then in turn halve these. It follows that halfway between north and east is northeast. Halfway between north and northeast is north-northeast. Halfway between east and northeast is, logically, east-northeast. And so on. This is close enough for most backwoods travel, although to pinpoint a direction you can always use the degrees themselves.

DECLINATION

Compass reading would be just this simple if it were not for the fact that the entire earth is a magnet, with one end at the magnetic north pole and the other at the magnetic south pole. What complicates all this is the fact that the magnetic north pole, which controls the compass, is situated some 1,400 miles south and east of the geographic North Pole off the polar coast of Canada.

This declination, marked on many maps, is necessary to know if you are traveling by map or by natural signs, such as those influenced by the sun. But it is not necessary to have a map to learn the declination in your area. The North Star is always within about one degree of true north, near enough for all casual wilderness travel. Locate the North Star some fair night where you are camped, scratch a line or lay a pole or such pointing to it, and in daylight compare this to your compass needle. The difference is close to the local declination.

One other consideration in this matter of declination may be important. Although the compass needle will generally tend toward the magnetic north, it will in practice show the direction of the most powerful local magnetic influence, wherever that may be. The most troublesome factor is natural ore deposits. Other elements are flashlights, the photo-electric cells

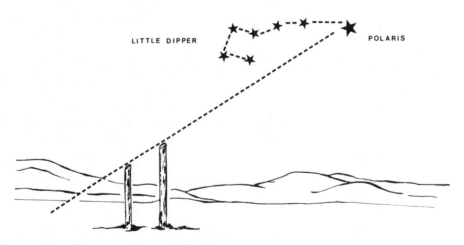

Using the North Star to Fix North

Finding north by this self-explanatory means is more complicated than other methods, but far more precise. The sighting over the two poles is arrived at by trial and error.

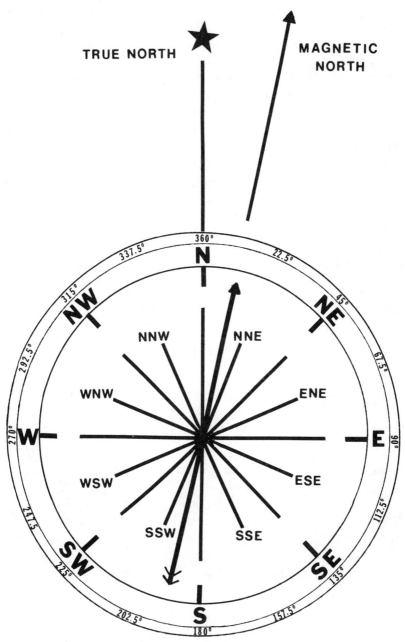

Using the North Star and a Modern Marine Compass to Determine Magnetic Declination

in exposure meters and in some cameras, power lines, gun barrels, metal fishing rods, battery-powered watches, etc. When taking a bearing, therefore, keep your compass as far as reasonable from such influences.

The North Pole and magnetic north coincide only along Florida's east coast, through Lake Michigan, and on up to near Bathhurst Island north of Hudson Bay. Everywhere else on this continent between this line and the Atlantic Ocean, the compass naturally points too far west; between the agonic line and the Pacific Ocean, the needle naturally points too far east. This is easy to remember if you fix the approximate position of the magnetic pole in your mind.

DIFFERENT COMPASSES

There are three major types of compass.

Type One, the most common, has a cardinal point and a 360°

system running clockwise from 0° north, plus a magnetic needle, ideally arrow-shaped or otherwise plainly marked to indicate north and turning independently of the dial.

Type Two is a compass on which the needle and dial are united and read together, usually also clockwise.

Type Three is based on a counterclockwise system of numbering the degrees and points. That is, north is still 0°, but the other degrees and cardinal points are read around to the left. The finest I own, a beautiful old British surveyors' compass of circa 1850-1880, with a clinometer for measuring angles of elevation or inclination, was made by F. Barner and Son of London for E. Esdaile Sidney and was presented to me by my friend J. F. M. Day. Jim, who is a licensed navigator, used one like it when a young man with the Coast Geodetic Survey in Alaska where, while keeping the camp in meat in addition to his surveying duties, he downed a trophy brown bear one memorable day.

Jim recently made me a gift of his rare and invaluable collection of compasses, among which is a superior example of one going back to George Washington's surveying days. His specimen of a case compass, really a museum piece, was carried by General Truxton Beale when he rode from California and Mexico to the president of the United States in Washington with the first news of Sutter's discovery of gold in California.

Let us consider the Type Three compass in detail, as it is used today by such professional outdoorsmen as surveyors, timber cruisers, and mineralogists, and by orienteers. It is my honor and pleasure that Jim Day, to whom this book is dedicated, consented to describe the use of the reverse-dial Type Three compass from firsthand experience. The following words are his. I could never have hoped to equal them.

"DIRAGO (Latin for: 'I point the way.')

"The Arabic word 'azimuth' means, literally, 'the way to go.' Since immemorial times the compass has been showing mankind 'the way to go'; yet I have noted numerous instances of would-be woods and wilderness travelers buying small, cheap pocket compasses without any knowledge of their local magnetic variation. Maps are always available showing these magnetic declinations known as isogonic and agonic lines and with variations ranging as great as 40 degrees. Such lack of knowledge would be disastrous, indeed rendering the compass of little more use than a rabbit's foot suspended from the nimrod's neck.

"Furthermore our alleged woodsman seldom understands what correction to make for east or west variations—does he add or subtract? The nascent navigator uses a variety of mnemonic tricks to remember, such as T–O–E–S, 'toes,' and *to obtain eastern variation subtract!* So, when he takes a bearing or azimuth on a sighting landmark, he must either add or subtract to obtain a true bearing. If he neglects this precaution in long distances, his navigation will go sadly amiss.

"These aforementioned difficulties are effectively obviated by the use, not of a small 'tin' compass customarily sold to tenderfeet, but by the purchase of the kind of compass used by professional travelers, such as foresters, timber cruisers, geologists, and explorers, the engineer's compass or pocket transit after 'Brunton.'

"Such an instrument provides that it may be set for local variation (indicated on every proper map) and then with its dial graduated in 360° running counterclockwise and the east and west letters on the face plate reversed, every bearing is a true bearing conforming to the geographic north and not the magnetic north.

"All the formerly bewildered voyageur has to do is to point the sighting device on the compass at his landmark and read the true bearing *off the north end of the needle!*

"Conversely in setting a course, the woodsman orients the pointers or sights of his pocket transit and then reads the true geographic course off the north end of the needle. For instance, if he wants to go straight east, he swings the north end of the needle to 'E' or 90° and the sights on the compass will indicate a true east bearing. If he should wish to go due south, he turns the compass till the north end of the needle is at the 'S' mark of 180°, looks along the sights, and he is headed toward Antarctica. To go west he would move the north end of the needle to 270°.

"In making these tentative operations in using an engineer's compass, it will readily be seen why the east and west

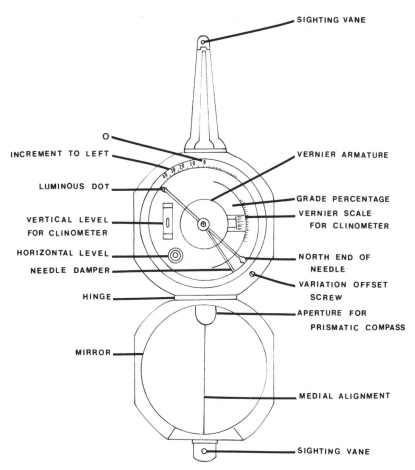

The Brunton or Pocket Transit
(Drawing by Vena Angier and Walton C. Titus)

This is the compass used by explorers, geologists, timber cruisers, rangers, archaeologists, and the U.S. Coast and Geological Surveys.

It is made of nonferriferous metals, and its closed lid protects it. When it is opened, sighting vanes or arms are exposed as in a prismatic compass. At one side of the Brunton is a screw head which rotates the dial, permitting the user to offset the reversed scale for magnetic variation. After the variation has been set for the relevant locality, the pointers or sighting vanes will indicate azimuths and the user then reads the *true bearings off the north end of the needle*.

The Brunton may be used to read horizontal as well as vertical angles. The instrument is equipped with a clinometer. Percentages of gradients may be read. The Brunton may be employed as a common military type of prismatic compass as well as a surveying level.

The more professional traveler or explorer may consult a table of logarithms affixed to the lid of this most versatile compass.

letters are always reversed on a pocket transit or Brunton. Also why the 360 scale runs counterclockwise.

"It is the simplest and best type of compass to use once the trick is mastered. Additionally, this type of compass is traditionally equipped with a level and a clinometer for measuring vertical angles and percentages of gradient.

Jim Day, Jan. 1977"

WHY EVERYONE NEEDS A COMPASS

Too many find their way through a certain area by familiarity. This is too restrictive a practice to be sensible unless one plans to stay in his own neighborhood all his life. Even then there will be occasions, as when a storm blots out surroundings, when at the very least a compass can save a lot of time, not to mention its benefits when one strays beyond his own locality.

Furthermore, as has happened to me, you may find yourself out later than you'd planned. On one occasion I recall, the overcast night was no more than thirty minutes away. From a knoll in back of our new cabin, I could see chimney smoke drifting upward from where I knew Vena had a moose mulligan simmering, perhaps a mile and a half away through a series of spruce swamps. Not taking declination into account, I could see that the familiar spot on the river was due south. So by continually checking my compass, I reached there in a straight line while I could still see obstructions such as eye-threatening branches ahead of me. This would not have been possible during the remaining dusk without a compass.

Too, I once climbed an almost sheer peak in the sheep country of the Liard River, where the only way of descent without ropes was precisely northwest. This was easy enough to see at the moment, and the time was midday. But before I could get around to climbing down, clouds of a fast-approaching weather front closed out all but immediate visibility. With my compass I cautiously and safely reached the mountain lake below where my outfit and horses, their leader belled, were waiting.

Who needs a compass? Everyone! This instrument need not be expensive, but it should be rugged enough to withstand moisture and hard usage. It should have a luminous dial, especially if there is some way of having this luminosity periodically renewed. Otherwise a cloudy night may lessen the effectiveness of your compass. This nearly happened once to me in the mountains of Idaho, when I had to get back to camp within a few hours to make necessary connections. Without a luminous compass, I'd have had to waste both time and otherwise-needed matches to keep located.

I prefer a small compass such as the recently developed luminous, lightweight Williams Guide Line Compass, inexpensively obtainable if not yet stocked by your dealer from the catalog-issuing Williams Gun Sight Company in Davison, Michigan 48423. This compass is waterproof, shockproof, so light that it floats, and filled with a liquid that won't freeze. Pinned to the outer clothing, it has the advantage of being less easily mislaid or lost. Best of all, the floating face remains always horizontal, ready for a quick check at any time.

Despite the usual preponderance of natural direction signs, both celestial and terrestrial, you may agree with me that in the real backwoods it is reassuring to always have a second compass. Mine is in the hilt of my Randall knife which W. D. Randall, Jr., P.O. Box 1988, Orlando, Florida 32802 made for me after extensive personal consultations and was kind enough to name the Bradford Angier Survival Knife, although I have never had any financial connection with him or it. Under extreme conditions, as in sheer wilderness, a spare compass proves to be as reassuring as the extra waterproof, unbreakable case carefully filled with strike-anywhere wooden matches that I always carry.

METHODICAL USE OF THE COMPASS

Too many people today look upon a compass as being something magic. They think that all they have to do is look at it

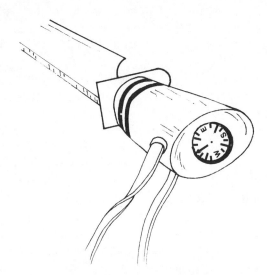

Bradford Angier Survival Knife

and it will automatically tell them how to get back to camp. This it will do, but only if it is used correctly. It must be so used from the moment you first leave your campfire.

If you are not using a printed map or paying any particular attention to such natural signs as the sun—a very bad habit to get into—it's entirely feasible to travel all day from the direct readings of your compass, not taking declination into account. If you head out in the morning by compass north from a compass east-west river, you can return by compass south. For practical reasons, however, as we'll consider in a moment, you had better return either slightly east or west of compass south so that when you reach the river you'll know which way to turn to reach camp.

First of all, whenever possible, you should camp by a long line that cannot be reasonably missed and whose general direction and length you have ascertained. This can be a large river (not a brook, where you may become confused by coming on a branch or similar stream); a road such as the Alaska Highway (one you definitely know does not come to an end within a few miles and one you will not sanely cross in a heavy snowstorm); the foot of a well-defined mountain range rising abruptly from a flat; a power line; or something of this sort.

Let us take the example I know best, the Peace River, a 2,200-mile-long wilderness thoroughfare which begins west of the Canadian Rockies where the Finlay River flows south along the Continental Trough and the Parsnip River runs north, meeting just below what was Finlay Forks and abruptly becoming the Peace River. The river follows, with some name changes, east into Great Slave Lake, from whence it slips as the notable Mackenzie River to the Arctic Ocean. The headwaters of this system have unfortunately been altered by the political damming of the Peace at Rocky Mountain Canyon. Where the dam extends is fourteen miles in a straight line from Hudson Hope, British Columbia, making a huge log-clogged lake that backs up both the Finlay and the Parsnip but which does not alter the direction-locating potential of the watercourse.

We originally built our log cabin on the sunny north shore of Rocky Mountain Canyon, five miles above the then tiny log-cabin settlement of Hudson Hope. No matter where we were, unless we managed by boat or ice to cross the broad river, we could always be sure of finding the cabin by hiking south to meet the watercourse and then, if we were not too exhausted, by following it to our cabin. In practice, because of the vastness of the distances involved, we had to pinpoint the cabin. In this lay the first shortcut of finding our way alone in the bush.

THE INITIAL SHORTCUT IN FINDING YOUR WAY

We are camped, for purposes of illustration, on the middle north shore of the unsettled Wapoose River somewhere in the grizzly country of the Continental Northwest. We have reached our tent site by boat. The Wapoose, we know from the map we have, runs some 100 miles from a fairly large mountain lake and is the only river of any size nearby. It runs from west to east, and we are about 50 miles from where it rushes into the Liard—certainly a long line at which to aim.

We are each proceeding on our own, you hunting and I

prospecting, although of course I'll gladly help you bring back any meat, and if you want the head and pelt, after you get it. But the first morning in this wilderness, absolutely strange to each of us, we each set out alone—you with your scope-sighted .30-06 Winchester Model 70 rifle which, with the 220-grain cartridges you are using, is big enough to bring down safely and surely any big game on this continent with an anchoring and killing shot one-third of the way down the foreshoulder of the animal, or in front halfway between the eyes and slightly high.

You set out north from our tent, across wind, at daybreak, which here is about 6 A.M. You want to be back by a safe 6:30 P.M. Thus by boiling the kettle for half an hour at noon, toasting your sandwiches and sipping your tea, you effectively divide the day in half. You don't know how far you have traveled north, but you can be sure that by returning at about the same pace during the remaining daylight you should safely reach camp by dusk.

Not having a detailed map, you draw one as you go, frequently turning to check the look of your back trail. This is flattish, wooded country. The prevailing wind continues to blow across you, which is good for all-day hunting. Checking your compass occasionally, you continue to travel in a fairly straight line by keeping two specific trees, and then two more, lined up most of the time ahead of you. You realize, of course, that with downfalls to skirt and small creeks to cross where comfortable, there is no such thing as a straight line in the forest. But by consulting your compass and allowing for zigs with corresponding zags, you keep traveling in a generally northerly direction.

Lunch over soon after noon, it's time to start campward. You know this lies generally south, but to hit it on the nose would be either a matter of luck or would have taken from the first a lot more reckoning than you had time for. By walking generally south by compass at the same pace you'll reach the Wapoose close to dinnertime, true. But then, not knowing the country, would you head up or down the river? Here's where that all-important shortcut comes into play to make your orientation simple.

You want to hit the river definitely a bit west or east of our tent. Because that very important hunting wind is still blowing from the west and because the going looks just as promising that way, you decide to reach the river upstream from our outfit. So you head south-southwest (see Map A). This will take a little longer, so you hasten your stride a trifle. You reach the broad Wapoose at 6:15 P.M. If you'd knocked over a grizzly and stopped to open him up, you'd have quickened your pace even more to allow for the delay. But you know for sure that camp lies a bit downriver. All is well.

REACHING A TRAIL GOING DIRECTLY AWAY

The preceding plan, whenever it will work, is the foremost stratagem for staying found in the wilderness anywhere. I have also used it a number of times—in Maine, Quebec, and British Columbia—for locating a trail leading directly away

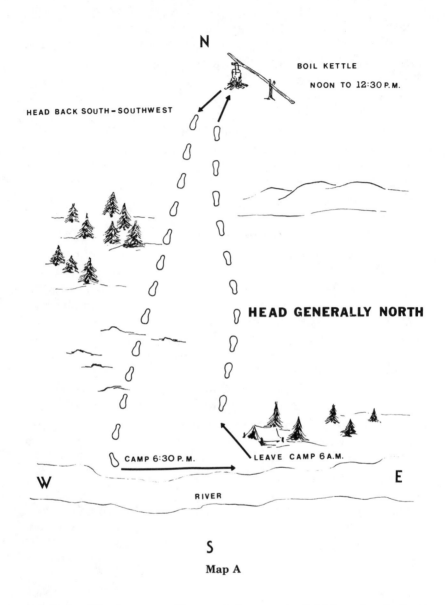

Map A

from me. The last occasion remains most vivid in my mind, so let us refer to it.

This took place across the Peace River from our cabin where, for several weeks earlier in the year, I'd been ferrying an acquaintance, George Waugh, and his survey crew for preliminary work in laying out some Crown Land for logging by a local friend, Earl Pollan. George and his men had bushed out several miles of the generally north-south Peace River Block Line, and I followed this on my look for a fat buck to help fill our cabin's meat cache for the coming cold weather.

I found my tender muley spikehorn unexpectedly in a sapling-filled field beside a fallen-in cabin. Neither of us had realized the other was nearby, and I dropped it with a brain side halfway between eye and ear openings from the side. I butchered and skinned it, enclosing the meat in a protective fabric sheath where it was safe from blowflies and Canada jays. I hung it in a shady, breezy spot until I could return in the cool of the evening to carry it, draped over my shoulders, to the boat.

By ten o'clock that morning I was continuing on my travels, it being much too fine a day to spend behind a typewriter. By far the easiest and quietest way to traverse this heavily overgrown and generally fallen-in country was along the brushed Block Line. So I continued to follow that slowly and comfortably for another two hours, using my binoculars and Leica frequently, until I reached a grassy spot, long ago cleared by fire set by the Moberly Lake Indians to bring in game, where there was a spring. Here I boiled the kettle. Bullhead Mountain, although across the river, was close to my northwest; ahead, to my south, was a small unknown lake which I figured I had time to reach and explore before commencing my homeward journey.

There was no longer any evidence of the Block Line on the now south slope, but I thought little of this because of an inch of tracking snow as, by compass and sun, I continued southward.

The sun was hot, and the west wind chinooky. When the time came to head back to the Block Line, no semblance of my back trail remained, for the snow had melted. To save myself a lot of trouble in getting back through that jackpot on the side down to the Peace, and in order to pick up the spikehorn without backtracking, I had to locate that narrow Block Line.

I could have headed due north by compass, sun, and wind with the hope of hitting the Line on the nose. Too much

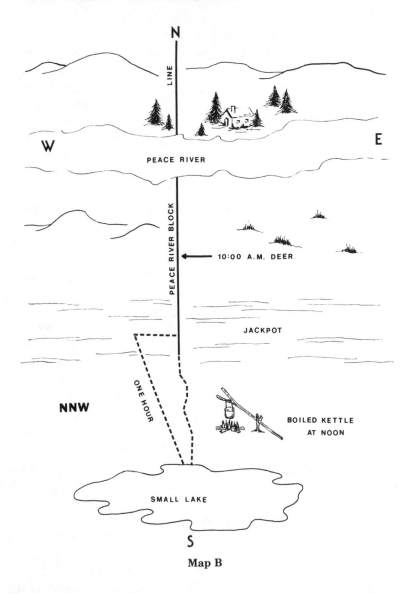

Map B

chance! I could have continued north to the crest, then started zigzagging northwest and northeast in widening traverses until I reached the trail. Not enough daylight! So, continuing to hunt for bear crosswind, I traveled a safe hour north-northwest through the erratic jumble of jackpot (see Map B), which by no means ended smoothly in an east-west direction.

By the time I was sure the elusive Block Line was a short distance east, I headed that way. My pattern worked.

THE SECOND BIG SECRET OF ORIENTATION

We are prospecting, this time moving our outfit with saddle and pack horses, in unknown, unexplored, and unmarked country three days east of the Alaska Highway. We have camped for a week in a meadow by one of several small streams, where the graze is particularly good, and we've hobbled and belled our half-dozen cayuses. It is flat, forested country without landmarks. How do we leave camp each morning with the certainty of returning safely by nightfall? Again the solution is a positive one. We keep from getting lost by staying found.

Our method takes time, but it will save considerable time and worry in the end. Carefully considering compass declination, which we check with the North Star, and using camp as the central point, we blaze four lines—north, east, south, and west—each some two miles long. To save additional time in such cases, the method I use is to put the higher of the two opposite blazes on the side of the tree nearer camp (*h* for *high* and for *home*). Such blazing, in effect, gives us a giant spoked wheel at which to aim. It isn't difficult to keep close enough tabs on our whereabouts during the day to be able to return to this blazed landmark toward evening.

This, of course, is a method that does not allow for many mistakes, or the course would be to head west for the Alaska Highway, in the meantime putting our companion through a great deal of work and worry. So we have arranged two things. If for some reason we are delayed one afternoon so that we might not return to the critical area while there is still enough light to find the blazes, then the only safe and sane procedure is to make an overnight camp wherever we might be and proceed the next morning. Furthermore, if one of us is ever in any difficulty and needs help, he is to fire three shots one minute apart, the answer to which is to be a single shot. Incidentally, we never have had to do either.

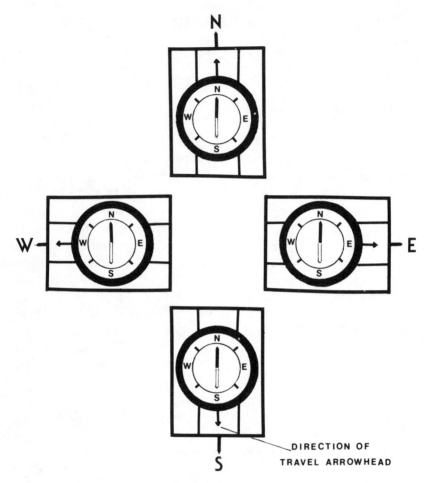

DIRECTION OF
TRAVEL ARROWHEAD

Using the Compass to Travel North, South, East, or West
To go in any of the four cardinal directions, set the base of the direction of travel arrowhead at the direction desired, orient the compass (i.e., have the master end of the needle pointing due north both in reality and per compass markings), and follow the arrowhead.

USING THE COMPASS WITH A MAP

Allowing for declination when reading a map is simple in the extreme. It is short-sighted and may lead to trouble in the future not to do it, particularly as a declination of only 15°

when not allowed for will put you a quarter-mile off course after one hour of travel. Instead, just lay the map flat on the ground or other level surface. First, roughly orient the map by placing the compass on it, then turning the paper until the north-south grid lines are parallel to the compass needle. Finally, for accurate adjustment, turn the map again until the compass indicates the amount of magnetic declination for where you are. For example, if you are in mid-Montana and the declination is 18° east, true north is not where the needle is pointing but 18° to the left of the needle. As we have seen

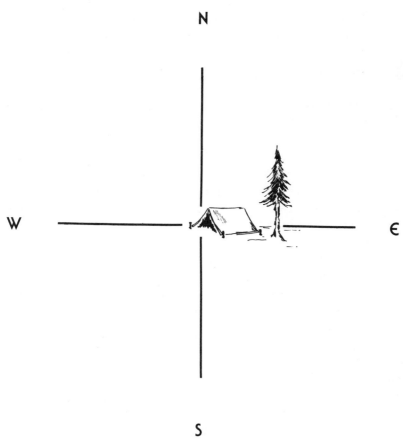

Finding Camp Through Blazes
Diagonal lines represent blazed trails.

with some of the more precise modern compasses (the Type
Three compass discussed earlier in this chapter), it is possible
to reset the bearings on the rim of the compass dial. Too,
special maps are regularly printed showing current compass
declinations.

AERIAL PHOTOS

Not even the best aerial photograph can take the place of
even a sketchy map. Used together, though, they can make an
excellent combination. When a map is both general and selec-
tive, the photo truly reveals all that can be seen from the air.

An aerial map, essentially, differs from a snapshot you take
of wild country only because it is photographed straight
downward, or nearly so, from a higher spot. Because of the
accuracy thus obtained, wild recesses throughout much of
North America have been mapped and opened to the master
outdoorsman. Simple to use, such maps enable more precise
journey-planning, then on the spot attain even more importance in that with care they can be read immediately in terms
of the actual country, showing exactly what to expect around
the next bend. The regular map is still needed for exact orientation and, of course, for explanatory names and scale. Then,
too, excessive bush and forestation often hide vital details
such as trails, trappers' and prospectors' cabins, and such, a
shortcoming that any cloud cover will exaggerate.

Aerial maps are available in groups. The flyer generally
works from west or east, thus keeping all shadows in the same
direction. After he has thus worked one edge of the desired
area, he makes a half turn and shoots his series of pictures to
show a corresponding and adjacent series from the opposite
direction. This pattern is followed until the complete target
area is covered. Or it should be.

Each photograph is then numbered with three desig-
nations: the mission identification, then the flight line, and
finally the individual nine-by-nine contract print number. By
using the compiled index, you can find the exact area or areas
in which you are interested. Plane and exposure speeds are

diligently controlled to get a sixty percent overlap on successive photographs, at the same time sidelapping by approximately half that distance to prevent gaps in any direction.

Scale, of course, depends on the height of the flight and the focal length of the particular lens and is generally noted in the index. As with any maps, the larger the scale the more detail and the smaller the region covered in each particular print. But, depending of course on your purpose, the added information is usually worth the extra expense of more prints.

Incidentally, check the filled order upon its receipt to make sure you have acquired what you want, best verified by first lining up the prints in sequence. Using a large flat area such as a bare floor, find key points in each picture and use these, always watching the shadows for maintaining precision and allowing for the handy overlaps, to number each print plainly for your future identification. A river, for instance, may help with this. Using a large sheet of transparent paper, perhaps made by several sheets joined with transparent tape, make your own detailed, photo-numbered map for future reference. When the time comes to store the prints, arrange them in sequence, place between two heavy pieces of cardboard (perhaps cut from a box), and put away in some place where there will be no extremes in humidity and warmth, keeping a large book or some sort of heavy object on them to combat the natural tendency to curl.

The way geologists and surveyors work is by using two sets of identical photographs with a legged stereoscope which, consisting of two lenses, directs each eye to a separate print, giving a three-dimensional effect.

Always line up the photos with the shadows of trees, cliffs, and such pointing toward you so that the result will not seem to be upside down. Use a key point such as a prominent crag to get lined up, moving the uppermost picture back and forth so that the pinpointed feature appears to drift together. Then, when the prints are correctly aligned some 2½ inches apart and the normal converging of the eyes conquered, the three-dimensional effect will abruptly come into being. This may take anywhere from a second to several minutes, although vision defects in some individuals preclude their ever achieving a stereo effect.

Relative to the image's position as regards the edge of the photograph, some curling upward, out of the way, of the uppermost print may have to be resorted to. This is apt to result in some confusion and manipulation until all is coordinated. Therefore, it's usually best to experiment first with your table stereoscope and a pair of familiar scenes. But the results, when you master the technique, will be astonishing, if perhaps overemphasized, until you get used to the overall effect.

You'll be better able to judge distances, too, once you've worked with a pair of familiar scenes. For instance, two lakes six inches apart on a pair of photographs with a scale of 1:12,000 would be a trifle more than a mile from one another, six times the scale of 12,000 inches or 72,000 inches. Transposed into feet by dividing by 12 inches, this gives 6,000 feet. A mile, as you know, is 5,280 feet. But you must always realize that only at the photo's center is the scale approximately correct. It all takes experience, but what it adds to the knowledge of unfamiliar country is infinite.

OBTAINING MAPS AND AERIAL PHOTOS

Maps detailing the wilderness in which you plan to be are nearly always both inexpensive and easy to secure. For anywhere in the United States, write for the free Topographic Map Index Circular of the state in which your interest lies and for the publication *Topographic Maps.* A postcard to the U. S. Geological Survey, Map Information Office, Arlington, Virginia 22202 will do.

The Index, which notes prices, shows a map of the entire area divided into quadrangles. Ascertain the quadrangle you need and, including a check or money order, request it. If it lies east of the Mississippi River, mail your order to the above address. For maps west of the Mississippi River, including Louisiana and Minnesota, write to the U. S. Geological Survey, Federal Building, Denver, Colorado 80225. This latter office also handles aerial photographs, topographic maps, and geodetic survey controls for each state, Puerto Rico, the Virgin Islands, American Samoa, and Guam. Most valuable are the available contour maps which—preventing a lot of unnecessary climbing and descending—show valleys, ravines, mountains, and other physical features in terms of elevation.

If you are writing from Alaska for maps of that state, address the U. S. Geographical Survey, 310 First Avenue, Fairbanks, Alaska 99701.

For regions not detailed in regular topographical maps, and for information concerning maps produced by government agencies, write to the National Cartographic Information Center, U. S. Geological Survey, 507 National Center, Reston, Virginia 22092.

Free price lists covering maps of all units of the National Park Service are sent from the Office of Information, National Park Service, Eighteenth and C Streets N.W., Washington, D.C. 20249.

Sectional maps, ordered from free lists supplied by the Superintendent of Documents, U. S. Government Printing Office, Washington, D. C. 20402 have long been available below cost.

Nearly three million maps and charts, thirty thousand atlases, several hundred globes and models, and a fifty-thousand card bibliography of cartographical literature are to be found in the Map Reading Room, Library of Congress, First Street and Independence Avenue S.E., Washington, D. C. 20540. Data on the ordering of both free and priced maps and other publications are to be found in *Library of Congress Publications in Print,* revised annually and available free from the Office of the Secretary of the Library at the same address.

Write for pamphlet FS-13 to the Forest Service, U. S. Department of Agriculture, Washington, D. C. 20259 for the addresses of the ten regional offices of the National Forest Ranger Districts, as well as other sources from which often free maps, strong on access roads and other man-made features, can be secured.

Canadian maps can be obtained from the government publicity offices in the provincial capitals, from the Government Travel Bureau in Ottawa, Ontario, and from the Map Distribution Office, Department of Mines and Technical Surveys, Ottawa, Ontario, Canada.

For government maps of Mexico, address your inquiry to the Direccion de Geografia y Meteorologia, Tacusaya, D.F., Mexico.

Private sources of both domestic and foreign maps include: The National Geographic Society, Seventeenth and M Streets, N.W., Washington, D. C. 20036, and the International Map Company, 595 Broad Avenue, Ridgefield, N.J. 07657. The Society's scope is well known, of course, while the latter company has a large stock of U. S. and Canadian topographic maps as well as maps of other countries.

For air photos, which ordinarily should be ordered at least half a year in advance, write for the free *Status of Aerial Photography* to the Map Information Office, U. S. Geological Survey, Washington, D. C., 20242. This publication indicates the availability and source of the government agency or private company holding the desired negative from which the order can be printed, all of which takes correspondence, identification, and time.

Excellent aerial photographs of the Dominion of Canada can be acquired from the Air Photographic Unit, Department of Energy, Mines, and Resources in the capital city of Ottawa, Ontario.

STAYING FOUND

With a magnetic compass and a map you should never become lost except as the result of an accident, such as being forced down in a plane in an unknown area. But when you are traveling on land from a definite spot, getting lost is an entirely negative thing. You become lost not because of anything you do but because of what you fail to do. In other words, you stay found by keeping track of approximately where you

are at all times. This takes a little time and effort. But far from being complicated in practice, the procedure becomes, instead, second nature.

You can stay located in any wilderness at any time— although, if only for safety, you should not travel at night except, perhaps, in the desert because of the coolness then—by means of a map, magnetic compass, paper, and marker. Every quarter hour or whenever you change direction (not including the practice of going around small obstacles, for which you can immediately compensate) will at first not be too often to bring that map up to the moment. No map? Then just sketch one as you proceed.

This is the sole and complete secret. As you gain in experience, you'll find yourself doing more and more of this mapping in your head, that's all.

DIRECTION-FINDING WITHOUT A COMPASS

There are many ways of getting along without a compass although, while often more accurate than the magnetic needle, they usually make the going unnecessarily difficult. Most of these methods have to do with astronomy, for even the sun is a great star. It is the reason why snow tends to be finer and less granular on the north sides of ridges and trees and such; why poplar trees have their darker sides on the north; why solitary coniferous trees tend to be bushiest on the south; why the age rings of trees that have been growing in the open are ordinarily widest on the southern side; why north slopes are less dense and more easy to travel through than the bushier south sides; why ant hills are always on the warmer south sides of rocks and similar objects; and on and on.

Because the sun rises and sets due east and west only two times a year, and then only over flat country, it is only at midday by sun time that it precisely tells direction throughout the year. If before noon you push a slim, straight stick into the ground and, with a thong or a vine perhaps a yard long, draw an arc around it, using the stick's shadow as the radius, you will be able to determine exact direction. Put a peg or

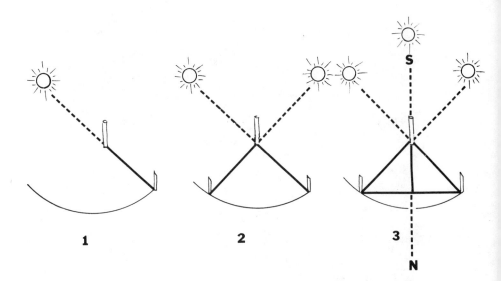

Using Sun, Stick, and Shadow to Find North

pebble where the shadow of the pole is touching the circle. When the pole's shadow next reaches the arc, mark that spot, too. Connect the two points with a straight line. A line from the stick to a spot halfway along the connecting straight line will point precisely north.

FINDING EAST BY SUN OR MOON

When the moon or sun is bright enough to cast a shadow, a quicker way exists to ascertain direction. Press or drive your straight stick into the ground as before. Mark the tip of its shadow. A few minutes later, mark the tip of the new shadow. A scratch joining the first mark with the second will point generally east.

Near noon with the sun and about midnight with the full moon this procedure is amazingly accurate. It is somewhat inaccurate during other times, but during a day of travel these inconsistencies will average out.

CHAPTER 8

Backpacking Back Of Beyond

It is still possible to backpack in the silent places for weeks at a time and have the time of your life with no more than a 35-pound pack, fishing essentials which need be only a few small hooks and a line, and a provision-lightening book or two like my all-color *Field Guide to Edible Wild Plants* and recipe-filled *Feasting Free on Wild Edibles*.

Realistically, this time can be prolonged by arranging with a bush pilot to drop sundries on a very carefully mapped and followed schedule or to plan for food caches to be left ahead of time, safe from wild animals, by a trapper or riverboat sourdough. But you'll have to deal with someone who is reliable, plot everything minutely, and be self-reliant. You can prospect along the way and maybe make a fortune, but best of all you are entirely footloose and independent (depending of course on whether or not you arrange for food drops or caches), free to roam and sleep where you will, and away from the care and cost of boats, cycles, four-wheel drives, and pack animals.

"Hiking a ridge, a meadow, a river bottom, is as healthy a form of exercise as you can get," said long-time Supreme Court justice William O. Douglas, who kept at it for years and who added, "Hiking seems to put all the body cells back in rhythm. Ten to twenty miles a day on the trail puts one to bed with his cares unraveled. Hiking—and climbing, too—are man's most natural exercises. They introduce him again to the wonders of nature and teach him the beauty of the woods and fields in winter as well as in spring. They also teach him to take care of himself and his neighbors in time of adversity.

"We need exercise as individuals. We need to keep physically fit and alert. . . . 'History is the sound of heavy boots going upstairs and the rustle of satin slippers coming down.' Nations that are soft and sleek—people who get all their exercise and athletics vicariously—will not survive when the competition is severe and adversity is at hand. It is imperative that America stay fit. For today we face as great a danger, as fearsome a risk, as any people in history."

Those who have never done any backpacking with modern equipment and improved methods have the idea that it is the toughest sort of work. In fact, many who have attempted such a vacation never repeat it because they have found it too much like toil. Yet any resemblance to hard work is usually due completely to improper equipment and incorrect technique. Done right, there is nothing hard about vacationing with a packsack. One can wander free and unfettered, with just enough exercise in the pure air to make existence completely enjoyable.

PROSPECTING FOR GOLD

There is still plenty of real wilderness in Alaska, the Yukon and Northwest Territories, elsewhere in northern Canada, and in many parts of the contiguous Unites States, which up to now have been comparatively overlooked. Start your imagination working, get out the maps, procure a book like my recent *Hunting for Gold,* which points out that many of this continent's great gold discoveries were made when the precious metal was selling for $20 an ounce. Then around 1936 there was a great surge of prospecting activity as the price rose to $35 an ounce. The increase to $38 a troy ounce in February 1972 brought a resurgence of interest. With the yellow metal now trading on the world market for premiums well in excess of the previously pegged prices, many a passed-over and forgotten prospect has become valuable. Thomas B. Nolan, as head of the U. S. Geological Survey,

opined a few years ago that possibly ten times as many new mining regions remain to be found in this country alone and, furthermore, that these should include as many primary areas as there are now. Despite all the prospecting of the past, vast districts, even those that are relatively accessible, have as yet scarcely been touched. This was proved in the great uranium rush in the early 1950's. How much chance does the amateur prospector still have? Well, in recent years more than 80% of the major finds of uranium and other radioactive ores have been discovered by inexperienced prospectors.

"The occupation of the miner is objectionable to no one," Agricola wrote centuries ago. "For who, unless he is malevolent and envious, will hate the man who gains wealth as if it were from heaven?"

American non-monetary consumption of gold has been three to four times greater than the domestic production for several years, and the United States is unlikely to become self-sufficient in gold in the foreseeable future. Non-monetary use of gold in the arts and dentistry and in industry for the fabrication of semiconductors, printed circuits, connectors, and other microcomponents for computer and space application is estimated at three to four times that of this country in the rest of the world. The point is, gold has no entirely suitable substitute for any of its major functions.

You can happen upon a gold strike while just plain hiking. You may find a placer, a water-borne deposit, using a frypan that has been burned free of grease in the campfire. In fact, the great *Pike's Peak or Bust* gold rush was begun in 1859 when George Jackson panned some dirt in no more than an iron treaty cup, one of those handed to the Indians in the region by the U. S. Government.

To start your own fortune-hunting, fill your frypan or whatever you're using about half full of gravel and sand, most promisingly dug as close to bedrock as possible. Now submerge it in water; still water, six inches to a foot deep, is best. Pick out the larger stones and pebbles by hand, looking for nuggets. Hold the utensil and shake it under water to allow the heavy gold to settle to the bottom. Tilt and raise the pan quickly, still under water, so that a swirling motion washes out some of the lighter top material. Keep this up with a rotary motion, lowering first one wrist and then the other, occasionally shaking the utensil under water or with water in it until only the gold and other heavy minerals remain, and sharply tapping it occasionally to help settle the minerals.

With proper manipulation, this material concentrates at an edge at the bottom of the utensil. Care must be taken that none of the gold climbs to the top or gets on top of the dirt. The process is repeated, slowly toward the end, until nothing is left but black sand and gold.

Nuggets and coarse colors of gold can then be readily picked out with a tweezer or a knife point. You'll probably find other minerals, too, and this can be important in the long run because the subsequent operation of the workings to remove such additional metals as silver and platinum may greatly increase the value of the claim. Collect samples and seek expert advice. If you suspect that you've found lode gold, chip off samples of unusual looking rock and then sack, number, map, and take them back to civilization for analysis and identification, conducted free by a number of government laboratories.

Always map and number, or otherwise identify, all samples of any sort so that you can return to any promising spot. All this adds the cayenne to the already enticing sport of backpacking in the wilderness where, too, the real trophies hang out.

APPROXIMATE BACKPACK WEIGHTS

Briefly, the total weight of the backpack for pleasurable mountain travel until one is experienced enough to judge his own capacity should not exceed about 35 pounds for young and active individuals. As for proportions, the equipment proper in the largest pack should not ordinarily weigh over 15 pounds, thus allowing a food load of at least 20 pounds. In these days of lightweight rations, one can take off for the backwoods for a month, and even this time can be stretched when rations are supplemented with wild edibles, like fish and berries and greens, as one treks along.

And so at the jumping-off spot, you shoulder your pack and head into the bush. You leave a lot of hustle and bustle—and expenses—behind. There is no other variety of vacation that can compare to these backpacking trips, none that can take you quite as close to serenity and utter freedom.

THE ONLY TWO SATISFACTORY PACKS

Only two packs are satisfactory today for this sort of vacation. The one still used for light loads is the Bergans type of alpine frame rucksack. This type of pack, usually with a single large and several smaller fabric compartments, is built around a strong, light, metal frame to which shoulder straps are attached to bear the brunt of the weight. Remaining weight is transferred to a band bearing against your hips. The packs are lightweight, relatively inexpensive, and wieldy,

neither snagging unreasonably on brush nor pulling you backward.

The best packs in the world for this type of recreation are variations of the old-fashioned Trapper Nelson type of packboard made in the United States and available from catalog-issuing outfitters and from stores throughout the country. Light, strong, and durable, the frames are usually made of tough aluminum tubing, although such metals as magnesium and stainless steel are among those also used. Two contouring uprights, following the shape of the normal neck, shoulders, back, and waist, hold the weight close to your body while keeping it forward where it pulls least against your bones and sinews. Like the functional old packboard, these frames will also hold game or such if the packbag is temporarily eliminated.

A lightweight two-inch web belt with its friction-held buckle tightly fastened will take nearly all the heft from the shoulders and put it where it belongs on the hips and strongly muscled thighs. A wide, padded harness yoke is also necessary.

For the packbag itself, get a large, rugged, waterproof-as-possible sack with a reasonable number of nylon-zippered pockets of tough, heavy-duty nylon duck fastened securely to the frame. A large pack will weigh approximately four pounds, the small only about a half-pound less. Deal with no less than the most reputable outfitter.

STOWING THE GEAR

With loads changing constantly as food is used, packing is a matter of day-by-day ingenuity. In essence, center your weight, except for padding the large pack with the softer articles such as clothing, and load high and near to the back, always keeping convenience in mind. Everything else considered, the first-used articles go in last. In stark, hot country and in rainy weather, this will be the plastic sheet or more durable poncho you may need for cover when you stop for lunch. Although you may find the contrary true for you, I like to strap my mummy sleeping bag, secure in a waterproof stuff bag, beneath everything.

In a party of two or more, the cooking utensils and other objects used in common, such as perhaps binoculars and camera equipment, should be fairly divided. Add a plate, spoon, and cup to the eating gear for each additional person. Stainless steel is better than aluminum for the plate and the cup, especially since the rim of the latter will be as cool to the lips as porcelain. For reasons of heat distribution and durability, the frypan should also be stainless steel. The remainder of the cooking outfit except for the tableware may well be lightweight aluminum. It should include at least two pots, both with bail handles, and a pan with a folding handle. All should nest within a zippered fabric container for cleanliness. Again, buy only the best. I bought such a nested outfit from Abercrombie & Fitch when first taking seriously to the woods forty years ago and it is still intact.

MUMMY SLEEPING BAG

In addition to its compactness and lightness, there are two reasons for selecting a mummy bag for your backpacking excursion. First, the volume of the bag which must be heated by the body is kept at a minimum. Second, the surface of the bag through which this heat is lost is also kept as small as possible. Thus, you have the warmest arrangement that is available.

Some individuals, such as my wife, take immediately to these form-fitting bags. In my own case, they took some getting used to. But nearly everyone who seriously tries one comes to like it, especially if the interior is made of hardwearing nylon, which makes for ease of movement and rapidly adjusts to body temperatures on even the coldest nights.

PLASTIC TUBING AS SHELTER

Plastic tubing provides a way to have a shelter for just a few pennies that's light to carry and quick to pitch. Just get a piece of plastic tubing about eight feet long, available at many outfitters. Put it up by running a rope through it as a ridge and tying the rope several feet high between two trees. No pegs are necessary, for the weight of the occupant anchors the tube. Such tubing can also be obtained in longer lengths, say fifteen feet, so that one camper can sleep at each opening and still have room for his duffle. An efficient insect defense can be fashioned at each opening from a few draped yards of bobbinet or cheesecloth. Dark netting is suggested for two reasons: it's easier to see out through, and the darker colors attract fewer mosquitoes and flies.

FOOTWEAR

There are several things to remember when buying footwear for the backwoods, all of which are based on the fact that one pound on the feet is comparable to five pounds on the

Shelter Made With Plastic Tubing

back. Although footwear will vary in conformity with use, one pair of leather boots should do for the entire trip. The boots should be sufficiently rugged to support and protect your feet with the heaviest gear you will carry. Your feet, accustomed as they have been during your lifetime to upholding your entire weight should, especially when toughened by usage, support you comfortably on a long hike even with thin soles and uppers, although the latter laces should be nylon, preferably braided for strength. Because of possible breakage and snagging, eyelets are superior to hooks. The fewer seams in the uppers, the more robust the boot.

The proved favorites among most trail veterans, particularly in the West, are the special boots, both domestic and imported, stocked by the big catalog-issuing sporting goods dealers for the express purpose of hiking over rough terrain. Equipped with the best of heavily lugged, thickly cushioned, rubber-and-synthetic soles, such as Vibram, these afford high traction and long wear. They are relatively safe, comfortable, and quiet, but not inexpensive. However, with reasonable care they are good for years, especially because they can be resoled when necessary.

If your sporting goods dealer cannot readily obtain these locally, it is practical to order them by mail, as a proper fit is guaranteed by the reputable firm. To measure your feet, put on the socks intended for the trail. Stand on a piece of paper on a hard surface, distributing your weight equally on both feet. Holding a pencil vertically, clearly draw an outline of each foot. Send these outlines to the outfitter, along with a notation of the length and width of your normal dress shoes.

Taking the thickness of your socks into consideration, here is a general rule to apply in selecting the ideal size of footwear for hard outdoor wear. With one pair of thin or medium wool socks, have your shoes one full size longer and one full size wider than your proper fit in city shoes. For heavy socks, have them one and a half sizes longer and wider. If half sizes are not available, increase to the next full size. However, there should always be as little motion as possible in the heels.

For the additional pair of socks that may be desirable in extremely cold weather, experiment to get the same comparative freedom of fit as above.

In the wet and swampy Northeast and in the Far Northern tundra, I like husky and roomy, eight-inch-high, leather-topped rubber boots worn with contoured and fleecy inner-soles and, except in warm weather, two pairs of good woolen socks. The type I have used all my life are the standards put out by the catalog-issuing L. L. Bean, Inc., Freeport, Maine 04031. This reputable family concern, started and operated for years by my friend Leon L. Bean and now by his grandson, L. A. Gorman, is still open twenty-four hours every day.

WOOLEN SOCKS

Regardless of heat or cold, dryness or dampness, only wool socks are suitable for long hikes, although you may like nylon reinforcements at the toes and heels to extend their lives.

These socks may vary from thin to medium during the summer, and from medium to heavy during the frosty months. Throughout the year, however, deal only with top-quality, finely processed, and well-made woolens. Don't have anything to do with shoddy ones if you can possibly avoid it. Poor woolens mat. They contain impurities that irritate the feet. They wear poorly. As for loosely and skimpily knit socks, these are an abomination from the first day one puts them on.

A few individuals are allergic to wool. Such hikers can often wear thin socks of some other material, such as cotton, under the wool as long as it is not slippery enough to bunch down toward the toes.

It should be noted that three closely packed pairs of socks afford less warmth than do two loose pairs. Aside from the fact that circulation is impeded by such a tight fit, the resulting compression of the fibers cuts down on the insulative dead-air space.

There is an entirely different way to combat cold feet, important inasmuch as the limits of effective insulation on the feet are rather quickly reached. This is one reason why the

answer to cold feet isn't necessarily thicker and warmer footwear. Oddly enough, it is an extra shirt or some other additional insulation around the waist, chest, and back that may warm the feet without any alteration of footwear. Depending on the requirements, the body is always regulating its heat, either warming or cooling itself. An accumulation of excess heat in the torso results in a cooling requirement. This is achieved by directing the overwarm blood to the extremities, which act as radiators. The effect can be concentrated in the feet by keeping the head and hands extra warm.

ADDING INSOLES

Insoles are frequently added to provide additional insulation, cushioning, arch support, and a more comfortable fit. They are most frequently made of leather, felt, or lambskin, all of which pick up moisture and should be taken out periodically for drying separately. They are also obtainable in woven synthetic fiber that is non-absorbent and non-matting and whose loose structure helps ventilate the feet.

BREAKING IN FOOTWEAR

It is very important that you break in new footwear well in advance of a trip. Some of us have feet that are abnormal in shape, probably because of improper fittings in city shoes. The lasts on which good outdoor shoes are made, changing as foot sizes have changed over the generations, are designed for normal proportions. When boots are new, even when correctly fitted, they may bring undue pressure on parts of your feet. The new footwear will gradually stretch at those points, however, if broken in slowly and easily.

There are two functional ways of breaking in new leather boots. It can be done gradually by hiking one mile the first day, two the second, and so on up to five miles—by which time the process should be completed. The second method consists of standing in four inches of water for fifteen minutes and then hiking until the shoes dry on your feet.

Never dry out your leather gear too rapidly, by the way.

Even the upper regions of a cabin or heated tent can become too hot from the sun or stove. Keep the leather supple and water repellent by dubbing it when it is clean and warm with a commercial compound, neatsfoot oil, or even the sourdough's bear grease.

FOOT CARE

BLISTERS

I always carry several small wrapped adhesive bandages in a pocket and apply one when a tender spot develops on any part of my foot, trying first to remove the irritant, which may be a thorn or bit of gravel. Felt moleskins, rather than rubber which may become too hot, are also helpful. These are simple adhesives, better than plain sticking plaster which has no cushioning effect. The moleskin can be cut to shape and the covering then removed. I try to keep one or the other pad on until the skin beneath hardens.

If a blister actually develops, it is most hygienic to leave it unbroken. If it has already burst, however, it may be advisable to trim away any excess skin that might cause additional irritation, wash with soap and water, and dry carefully. Keep such medicinals as alcohol and merthiolate off open blisters. These are skin disinfectants, not wound disinfectants. They kill delicate tissue and, while reducing the germ count initially, they harm the tissue. Germs multiply best on injured tissues, so you can see that you actually foster infection rather than reduce it with the use of these so-called disinfectants. Soap and water are best for cleansing a wound.

BLOOD UNDER NAIL

The pressure of blood under a toenail, perhaps the result of jamming a toe or having something fall on the foot, is a common source of discomfort. Pressure can be lessened by twirling a pointed knife over the center of a nail discoloration until blood seeps out of the hole. Although the knife should be clean, do not cauterize it in flame or you will take the temper out of the blade. Because the nail is lifted from the flesh by the blood, there is no danger of drilling into the flesh if you proceed cautiously. It takes only gentle pressure. Let the point do the work, and do not press hard on the blade.

WASHING

Care of the feet is fundamental on a backpacking trip. I find it refreshing—unless temperature, water, or time makes it impractical—to wash my feet at midday. I also wash my socks, particularly if they are perspiration-soaked, and dry them when practical by tying them to the outside of my packsack.

Wool responds well in cold water to regular soap if care is taken and the socks are pressed (not wrung) free of water and dried slowly. Detergent extracts important oils from the material and should not be used. Rinsing is better than nothing if soap is not handy. Dirty socks abrade, and they insulate poorly, in part because they can no longer absorb the usual amount of perspiration. When for any reason it is not convenient to wash or rinse socks when changing them on the trail, I relegate them to a separate plastic sack and stow them safely inside the pack until I make camp.

HIKING TIPS

In making time, a sound formula that I have proved to my satisfaction over the years is never to step on anything you can step over, and never to step over anything you can step around. As for rests during the journey, many find it beneficial to take it easy for about five minutes each hour, if only by leaning against a tree or ledge so that the weight of the pack is lessened. Never tarry for longer under ordinary circumstances, however, or your muscles may stiffen unnecessarily. A sound rule is to start walking again while you are still warm.

Getting into your pack? Obviously the best way is to lean the load against an elevated stump, bank, or rock so that you

can get into it at shoulder level. Otherwise, unless it is light enough or you are adept enough to get one strap into position and then to swing the load around to the other shoulder while erect, place the pack upright on the ground, sit down, shoulder it, and then stand, tightening the waist strap to the desired degree while you are erect. For fullest support, the strap will be on the snug side.

CHAPTER 9

Paddling Your Own Canoe

This continent's Indians developed bark canoes, the forerunners of the present water craft which have never been equalled in their universal efficiency for stream and lake travel, by using chestnut, elm, cedar, spruce, hickory and birch barks. The toughness, pliability, and lightness of birch bark soon proved it best for the purpose.

Today the elegant, responsive, relatively safe and rugged, and easily maintained aluminum canoe merits the satisfaction that keeps it outselling all other canoes in the United States by five to one. Most popular in Canada, though, and accounting there for four out of every five sales, is the canvas-covered, cedar-strip canoe. And then there's fiberglass. All the exciting new canoe shapes—slimmer, lower freeboard, faster, easier to control in wind, sleek, and beautiful—are fiberglass.

If you want durability, buy aluminum. For speed and easy handling, get the competitively priced plastic craft, always bewaring of so-called *budget* canoes. For tradition and beauty, the canvas-and-wood crafts are supreme. In any event, purchase only the best, as a good canoe never depreciates more than about fifty percent. And so the debate goes on, but whatever choice the American or Canadian finally makes, one thing is certain—the North American backwoods are filled with canoeing waters to satisfy every taste!

"To have commanded the paddle, tasted the wind, and challenged the river—one would have believed that the splendor of God's wilderness is reserved for the canoeist." So George Washington Sears, better known to the Indians by the name of Nessmuk, wrote in 1888. "My own load, including canoe, extra clothing, blanket-bed, two days' rations, rod and knapsack, never exceeded 76 pounds, and I went prepared to camp out any and every night. . . . My canoe is my yacht, as it would be if I were a millionaire."

With a light canoe and outfit, one or two individuals can today go far back of beyond for several months at a time by living largely off the land with rod, gun (where one is legal), and edible wild fruits and vegetables. Here are the basic facts.

WHICH PADDLE?

It all starts with the painstakingly selected canoe, by means of which we can invade the deep wilderness for weeks at a time with more of an outfit than it would be possible to carry any other way than by pack animal. Second comes the paddle.

In all active sports, the difference between a good and an inept performance often starts with the choice of the specific tool that is essential to the activity. With canoeing, it's the paddle that is all important, particularly since during the usual day of cruising the ordinary North American outdoorsman will average about a stroke every two seconds, 30 a minute, 1,000 an hour, and close to 15,000 during a bracing day. This works out to something less than 500 strokes an average mile.

There is one beguiling fact, though, gleaned from the Indians. A short, quick stroke covers more miles with less effort than the more customary pace of some 25 to 30 strokes a minute. Try increasing the stroke to more like one every 1 1/3 seconds. Accomplishing this, the Indian centers his power in the first portion of the stroke. The strength he exerts falls off rapidly once the paddle is opposite his side, and he ends the stroke quickly after this point is passed. Actually, with a suf-

ficiently limber paddle, the swing of the blade and shaft will do much to shoot the paddle forward for the next stroke, and there should be a short surge of renewed power immediately before the blade leaves the water.

No matter what the technique, the paddle balance, shape, grip, weight, material, finish and, particularly, length are especially important. Initially, the paddle should fit the job, whether for bow or for stern. For work forward in the canoe, where little if any steering will ordinarily be done, the paddle should reach from the floor to the chin when the standing canoeist holds it upright. The stern paddle should be at least eye high. There are those, too, who like this master paddle in particular to be a couple of inches longer than standard depending largely on the lines of the specific canoe.

The most important thing about a canoe paddle is seldom mentioned. That is, the paddle should be long enough so that the user does not have to curve his back downward for the stroke. Basic canoe paddling is done by swinging the hips and shoulders so that the big muscles of the legs and back do the work smoothly. What is not wanted is hunching at every stroke. If you paddle kneeling, the correct paddle length for you will be different than if you stroke from a seat.

A third paddle for possible emergency use in every two-man canoe, a second if you are alone, should be included. It's easy to lose a paddle and possible to break one, and this spare should be carried handily under the load lashings where it may be grasped in an instant. If two individuals are about the same height, the length of the spare can well be a compromise between chin and eye measurements.

The canoe will travel faster and answer steerage demands quicker with a wide paddle. Conversely, it takes more power and endurance to draw a wide paddle through the water than it does to handle the often sufficient narrow blade. The actual widths in the stores today generally run between 5½ and 8 inches. By the way, if one of the blades selected is wider than the other, it should be in the stern paddle. When it comes to handling a paddle, much will depend on your own muscles and physical condition. The American Indians preferred the less tiring narrow blades.

Because of potential slipperiness and blisters, it's a sound idea to take any finish off the grips and shafts with sandpaper and if necessary a hardware-store solvent, leaving the original varnish to protect the blade. Thoroughly soak the wood that has been bared so as to raise the grain. This should then be sanded smooth. Continue until the wood remains smooth after soaking. Once everything is again dry, slick the hands with linseed oil and rub this into the shaft and grip. Backwoodsmen to whom this may not be readily available sometimes use bear oil instead, but the drawback to this is that it makes the wood more appetizing to gnawing porcupines, mice, and their compadres.

PADDLING

The canoe is afloat. You hold your blade and, because you are alone, kneel slightly to one side and just far enough back that the bow is slightly raised. You are now in control, ready to propel the craft ahead, to turn it sideways, to drive it backward, or to spin it so that the stern and bow are quickly reversed.

Everyone knows how to hold a paddle, one hand grasping the grip at the end and the other held partway down the shaft near where it widens into the blade. The lower hand should be kept high enough to stay out of the water. The grip is shifted to the right hand on top when you're paddling on the left. The left hand is above when you change your efforts to the right side of the canoe.

The blade is held at right angles to the craft. Then, reaching forward only so far as is comfortable, you swing the blade down into the water and draw it back, propelling the canoe forward. The upper hand continues to push while the lower, extended, serves as a pivot to the lever action. For the utmost power in return for the least effort, both arms should be

straight. Many find such a practice tiring, however, and let the arms bend naturally as they paddle.

Bring the blade back nearly vertically until it reaches a position opposite the hip. Do this by pushing with the upper arm, not pulling with the lower arm. Then lift the paddle out with the lower hand, at the same time dropping the upper hand toward the waist so that the blade floats upward and leaves the water.

All-important now that the stroke is completed is to rest both arms, an action so relaxing that it will be possible with a little practice to paddle all day without becoming more than pleasantly weary.

Bring the blade back for another stroke, turning it parallel to the canoe so as to minimize air and water resistance. Complete all this with the hands and paddle close to, but not scraping, the side of the canoe.

Your stroke should be completed smoothly and comfortably, with the entire body contributing to the easy and thus enduring power—an attribute that with practice will finally come naturally.

THE BASIC STROKE

When two people are paddling, each works on a different side of the craft. The canoeist in the stern, because he can see better, ordinarily adapts his position to that of the bow paddler. The individual in the stern, however, is captain and may direct the bowman with voiced commands, especially when running rapids.

With two paddlers, each working from a different side, the direction the canoe takes tends to equalize. However, the stern paddler ordinarily has to take special pains to keep it straight. This he may do by twisting the paddle when it is opposite his hip, turning the blade's inside edge backward, and bringing the paddle's flatness parallel to the canoe. The paddle thus serves as a rudder, and it takes little effort to give it a final push to one side or the other to keep the canoe on the desired course.

When you're paddling alone, this basic stroke will keep the

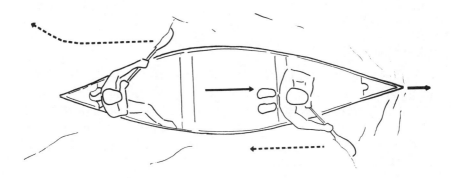

Basic Stroke

canoe moving smoothly and continuously in the desired direction no matter on which side you paddle.

GUIDE STROKE

Another method for directing the canoe ahead by stroking smoothly parallel to the craft without being distracted by the curve of the gunwale is the guide stroke. This stroke varies from the basic stroke in that at the end the blade is brought back underwater feathered—that is, held parallel to the side of the canoe—to a point opposite the hip where it is lifted. Thus, once more, the paddle works like a rudder.

This stroke differs among canoemen. One practice that sacrifices a certain amount of impetus is to hold the blade at a slight angle during the entire sweep, then to make the final correction during the quick upward flip at the conclusion, during which the gunwale may serve as support for the final pressure. Both variations, although they take practice initially, can be maintained for hours without undue fatigue.

BACKING STROKE

The fundamental forward stroke, whichever you find easiest, should be mastered first, for it is this that will be used most during your enjoyable hours of canoe travel. When the time comes to slow, halt, or back, merely reverse the cruising stroke.

JAM STROKE

To stop abruptly, plunge the blade into the water at right angles to the canoe. It will be easier to hold it there if you hunch forward over the shaft, pressing it tightly against the gunwale with the lower hand. For maximum efficiency and balance when two are paddling one canoe, apply the jam stroke together on signal.

TURNING THE CANOE

The handiest stroke to master is the one used for ordinary cruising. This stroke makes good sense throughout, whatever variation is used, and skill will come with practice. The other strokes depend on common sense, too, and even the untutored canoeist will find himself practicing most of them without any prior instruction when he needs, for example, to swerve or to turn. Yet for the utmost efficiency it is best to know the most practical time-saving techniques because in rapids, for instance, wasted motions may be perilous.

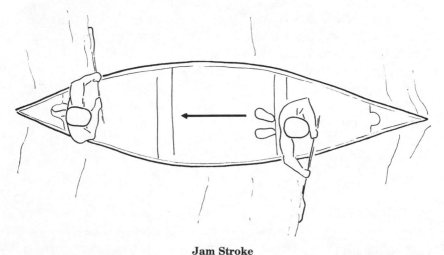

Jam Stroke

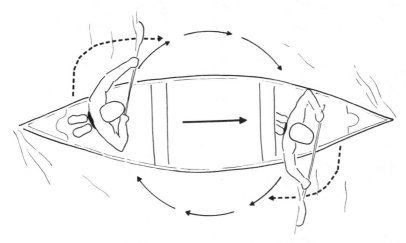

Pivoting a Canoe Within Its Own Length

To turn the canoe, swing the paddle like an oar out from and back to the gunwale in a circular sweep. Practiced on the right side of the craft, this will turn the canoe to the left. The same action can be accomplished by a full reverse sweep on the left side. The reverse sweep, of course, starts in back of the canoeist and completes itself in a half circle in front of him. Shorter sweeps can be used when the turn is to be less abrupt or when there is more time in which to complete it.

When there are two paddlers and each completes a full forward sweep on the same side of the canoe, the canoe will swing widely away from the paddles. To pivot a canoe within its own length, the stern paddler can perform a forward sweep and the bowman a reverse on opposite sides.

DRAW AND PUSH STROKES

The draw stroke, used to turn a canoe broadside, is accomplished by reaching straight out from the side with the blade at right angles to the craft and drawing the paddle straight back toward you. Two paddlers doing this from opposite sides will pivot the canoe abruptly.

The push stroke is merely the reverse of this, starting from the paddler's side and pushing straight outward. The same

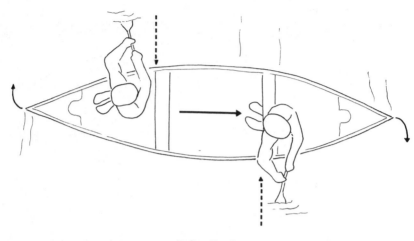

Draw Stroke

result, of course, can be achieved with a draw stroke on the opposite side, but there is not always time to shift grips. Again, two canoeists using a push stroke on opposite sides will rotate the craft.

Abruptly setting over a bow or a stern, depending on which of two paddlers applies it, the push stroke is most effective when the shaft is held against the gunwale and pulled swiftly and strongly inward. Such a dramatic stroke, which can break an inferior paddle, is usually saved for white water.

THROW STROKE

The throw stroke, used by the bowman, should be given a considerable amount of practice, preferably at low speeds in safe water. Caution is always called for. If the momentum is too swift at the moment of the stroke, the paddle can be wrenched under the craft and the canoe capsized; the paddler can be yanked into the water; or the paddle, if weak, may break.

Throwing the canoe is based on the fact that less momentum is lost on short turns if the bowman at that instant becomes the steersman. His paddle is held perpendicular in the water, close to the gunwale, with the forward edge of the blade straight ahead. If his wrists and arms are strong enough, the bow can be lifted and quickly thrown over to the opposite side, perhaps to elude a rock, by turning the leading edge of the blade toward the canoe. The paddle thus acts as a rudder, and it must be gripped staunchly because of the ensuing wrench.

Practicing these basic strokes so as to become adept with them in all conditions of water and wind makes the skillful, contented, and safe canoeist.

POLING

The use of a setting pole is greatly restricted by the kind of water in which it is used. The pole works best on a shallow, rocky stream like the enticing Grand Cascapedia River in Quebec's Gaspé Peninsula where, as stages of water lower, it becomes increasingly difficult to paddle.

On streams much over four feet deep, such as British Columbia's Peace River, the depth of the water is too great. Here, except along some of the shallower stretches, thrusting a pole in and pulling it out to reset becomes too cumbersome. On the other hand, on many of the streams of New England, especially Maine's, poling conditions are just about perfect.

An advantage poling has over paddling is in upstream work where, even when you are alone, you can exert nearly continuous power. The only time you lose control of the canoe is for the moment it takes to reset the pole, and even then you generally have momentum. With two persons there really can be continuous power.

The pole should be about 12 to 14 feet long, with an average taper of some 1½ inches. The seasoned wood is best peeled, then smoothed with a knife. It will be easiest on the hands if left in its natural state, although there are some who like to rub in boiled linseed oil. However, you'll likely find that the oil accumulating from your bare hands will be sufficient.

Poling techniques are best learned by practice. Pick a shallow stream, up which the canoe might otherwise have to be lined or portaged, and pole up it. Or first get the feel of the pole along a shallow lake shore.

Although one-legged outdoorsmen such as my departed friends Jim Beattie and George Crosman poled from a sitting position, by far the most popular stance is standing in the stern for one person and in both stern and bow for two canoeists. The canoe should be balanced, with the bow riding a bit higher than the stern. To accomplish this, the lone poler may have to stand near the center of the craft with one leg braced against a thwart. Otherwise, with two workers, the master should stand slightly off center in the stern with the back leg braced against the seat or rear thwart.

Although, as in paddling, you can pole from both sides, the most powerful thrusts are made when the master leg is advanced. Stand facing forward with your feet comfortably apart and parallel to the keel. As in riding horseback, there should be give in the knees, which should be partially relaxed but still springy.

Start in this position by holding the pole with the master hand near the top and the other hand about a foot and a half below. Set the pole close to the canoe and just in back of the rear foot. Then, being sure to stay balanced and well braced, push. As the canoe heaves forward, continue the thrust by climbing the pole hand over hand. When reaching the top of the pole, give the pole a final firm shove so as to continue the momentum while shifting the hand back down toward the middle and resetting the point in the waterway's bottom.

Direction is best controlled by the push itself, not by the later resistance of the pole to the stream as might be presumed by paddling techniques. As a matter of fact, the pole should be lifted completely clear of the water before being replanted.

Rhythm, which will come with practice, is important. Keep the bow pointed into the current, the canoe generally parallel to the shore, and in shallow enough water so that the bottom can be easily reached. Seek the quietest water where there will be the least pressure from the current. Often, in fact, it

Poling a Canoe Upstream

will be possible to find backwaters where the water is actually
swirling upstream.

Sometimes the pole will be caught between two rocks. Try
to jerk it free. If this fails, release the pole before capsizing
and return to it by paddle or by wading.

That's all there is to poling. But it's hard work, although
usually not as difficult as portaging the canoe and duffle,
which might have to be done otherwise. Skill comes with
practice, and it is encouraging to note that it is usually more
easily achieved than mastery of paddling.

MINIMIZING HAZARDS

Most individuals fear the possibility of capsizing in a canoe. This can certainly happen. In the normal sitting position on the seats, the center of gravity is higher than in any other boat and, of course, the canoe will go over easily due to its roundness. However, if the paddler sits or kneels on the bottom, the center of gravity will move well below where the center point of the roll is located.

All the tricky basics should be learned beforehand. Greenhorns, for example, do not realize how cold most of the canoeing waters on this continent are or how very quickly the immersed individual loses the ability to function. This happens all the time to inexperienced canoeists who are on mountain streams in the summer.

The day is hot; the stream a cool 45° or so; while shooting a rapids they go overboard, try to swim the rest of the way through while holding onto the stern or bow, and become so numb that they're in trouble. It's been in their minds that because it's July or August the water will be warm.

Most, too, do not appreciate how frail a canoe can become in big water when the wind starts to blow. In a banana boat or a decked canoe, it is possible to last through a hurricane. In an open canoe that's heavily loaded, trouble starts when the waves get as little as a foot high. Quckly there is a bailing situation, at the same time that all-out attention is needed just to handle the craft.

There is a sea adage that the time to take all precautions for the safety of the ship is when one *can* take precautions. This is particularly applicable to canoes, for they are essentially fragile crafts. It isn't going to take much in the way of difficulty before you lose the ability to do anything except bail or pray. Don't attempt to cross big water, such as lakes, but rather skirt the shores. Anticipate a potentially bad situation far in advance. By the time the rapids or storm has gripped the craft, it is too late. There's then not much the inexperienced individual can do. Taking precautions means looking well into the future and avoiding risk situations. The canoe is a magnificent craft, but it isn't very forgiving.

OVERLOADING

The most common cause of boat accidents is overloading, and this applies in particular to canoes. For long cruises on which heavy loads are nearly unavoidable, especially when you head out, both weight and bulk can be cut by substituting the modern freeze-dried foods for canned grub, by taking along in sheer wilderness the usually adequate tarpaulin or Whelen Lean-to Tent for shelter, and by determinedly eliminating equipment which is not essential. As with all travel, the more skilled and experienced the canoeist, the lighter his gear.

WHEN TO STAND IN THE CANOE

The best way when afloat to make a quick survey of the rapids you are about to shoot is by standing. This is also the most satisfactory procedure for spotting obstructions in shallow water. Canoe fishermen can get added distance in their casts if they are erect. Too, standing in a canoe is almost a necessity when poling. For enticing, refreshing pleasure while paddling along an enchantingly quiet shore, try it standing. The often-repeated axiom that one should never stand in a canoe is heard only from inexperienced individuals.

PAINTER NEEDED

Every canoe should have a painter, a tethering rope perhaps 20 feet long, fastened to the bow. When the canoe is brought ashore, this painter should be tied to an anchor such as a rock or tree. Otherwise, a rise of water might well float the craft loose, or a gust of wind might blow it adrift. Canoes are so light, especially in relation to their broad, sail-like surfaces, that this danger is a very genuine one, and more than one canoeist has suddenly stared over his campfire to find himself marooned.

STREAMSIDE REPAIRING

You should always carry one of the small, inexpensive repair kits designed for your particular type of canoe. With one of these, comparatively minor streamside remedies are easy. Otherwise, improvisations may become necessary, limited only by ingenuity and materials at hand. For example, in a pinch a canvas canoe can be patched with a piece of duffle bag or clothing, held on by melted or chewed conifer pitch in which, ideally, a small portion of bacon grease and a bit of charcoal from the campfire have been mixed. Small holes, too, can be patched with chewing gum, manufactured or wild, or with plain electrician's tape, preferably plastic.

Marred aluminum canoes should have all metal surfaces flattened out as much as possible. At the point of the injury that is to be repaired, the metal on both sides should be roughed, as with a knife tip. Then the tear or puncture is covered with fiberglass and saturated with epoxy resin. A kit

for emergency repairs should include a square yard of 10-ounce cloth, a pint of epoxy with hardener, and a knife for cutting the cloth and spreading the resin.

Fiberglass is prone to shatter, so it is fortunate that permanent repairs can be made streamside. First, dish out the break or puncture in concave fashion, using a wood rasp. Lay the first layer of 10-ounce glass cloth in the depression. Paint can be removed by rasping and polyester used as the adhesive, as it sticks well to glass. Some care must be taken that the resin doesn't seep away, and this is prevented by backing. After the concavity is built up, cut one or more patches in ever-increasing sizes. Two patches are a minimum, but no more than three are needed. The resin soaks in more evenly after the first patch. Fiberglass can be repaired with the startlingly strong epoxy by anyone who does not forget the hardener, a common mistake. Just slurp it on and grind off the crudity later.

FLOTATION

Good canoes will have plenty of built-in flotation, but off-brand boats should be inspected closely. Canvas and wood craft, of course, will not sink of themselves because of the inherent buoyancy of the wood; aluminum and fiberglass boats will not sink because of flotation substances or chambers built in their hulls.

As in all boating, no one should ever be allowed to leave a swamped canoe and swim for shore even when land may seem absurdly close. The procedure is to swim the canoe toward shore.

LIFE PRESERVERS

Do swimmers need to be concerned with lifesaving devices? The answer lies in the fact that the greatest number of drownings have taken place among good swimmers. When all is said and done about the life preserver, the most important consideration is that it be within easy grasp when it's needed. Again, always in the backwoods, hope for the best but prepare for the worst.

The flotation device each canoeist depends on should have sufficient buoyancy to keep both neck and head above water. It should be comfortable and easy to don and remove, at the same time allowing freedom of movement in and out of the water. It should not have any tendency to turn and press the wearer in a face-down position. It should have the characteristics of drying quickly and easily out of the water.

Especially for use in open water, such a flotation contraption is best when highly visible. It should be resistant to aging, weathering, extreme changes in temperature, and oil products. Its condition should remain evident through visual inspection. Such a personal flotation device, perhaps just a jacket like the one I use, should be bought to fit the individual and to be worn only by him, thus establishing both confidence and a sense of safety. Remember to put it on before you need it.

UP AND DOWN V'S

V's with their points upcurrent, directed toward the down-rushing canoe, are the enemies. V's where the wide angle is

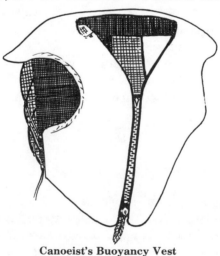

Canoeist's Buoyancy Vest

upriver open their arms for the canoe to glide through, and are friends.

The rock above water parts the current, making a white wave on either side that extends back past the rock in an ever-widening V like the wake of a ship. If the rock is below the surface, the V of the wake still shows. The deeper the rock, the further back from it is the apex of the V.

Time and experience tell the canoeist where and how deep the obstruction is by the tiniest of signals. Does the water bulge slightly in front of the V? Then there is ordinarily sufficient water to float the canoe over it. Is the bow wave a slow rumble that indicates deep water or an angry froth that means the rock looms close to the surface? Currents of varying intensities add to the difficulties of reading. A rock with 10 inches of water over it will give one signal in a current of 5 mph, another when the water flows at 10 mph, and no signal at all if the current is nonexistent.

Obviously, while the captain of the canoe (the individual at the stern is generally in command) avoids upstream V's, he seeks out downstream V's. Most rapids are a series of obstacles that obstruct the flow of water in a chain of haphazard, ineffective dams. Water will start flowing for the dam opening well upstream of it, gradually constricting until it reaches the opening. The telltale V upstream sweeps the canoe into the deep, safe slot.

HAYSTACKS

Haystacks are large standing waves that form where water suddenly rushes from a shallow section into a markedly deeper area. These waves do not change position like ocean waves but froth and boil constantly in the same spot. There is usually good deep water under them. They pose problems only when they reach such intensity and size that the canoe cannot plow through them without taking on an undue amount of water. If the bowman is a real expert, he will lean forward and flap his paddle from side to side to *flam* an open path through the frothy wave and help prevent this.

However, at times the waves become so big that they simply overpower any canoe not equipped with white-water decks. The boat hits a solid wall of water and scoops itself full even though it charges through the wave. Here, again, time and experience are the teachers. Although it is easiest to hit the haystack dead center because the current there is swiftest, those that pose threats must be taken on the edge, the canoe scraping past the rocks along the side if necessary to avoid the water well.

ACQUIRING RIVER KNOW-HOW

The stream in spring is a most benevolent teacher, and a most pleasant one, but only if the aspirant picks a gentle stream. The hours spent observing the play of the bottom surface in ever bolder versions are the least wasted of all. Is there a rapids by a nearby road where you can study this before you take to the woods? The budding canoeist can do worse than observe it through four seasons; in his canoe in gentle going, from the shore if weather and water turn unwelcome.

CAPSIZES

A vital rule to remember if your canoe does capsize is never to get downstream of it. Duck under it or hold position as it goes past. Also, swimmers are safer staying with a swamped canoe than abandoning it. The accepted procedure is to grab the stern and ride the boat down through the rapids as if swimming a horse, holding the stern to keep the boat straight.

Oddly, because of its now greater depth, the boat directed this way will in uncanny fashion seek the deeper water and often glide through bad stretches with amazing ease. If the canoe cannot be caught, swimmers should if possible head downstream on their backs, feet first, treading water until a calm is reached.

Often canoes become trapped against rocks and must be

Swimming a Canoe Downstream

manhandled off. Small saplings can be cut to serve as levers when the water is shallow. Ropes can be tied together and to a tree, and a Spanish windlass set up. Usually, a couple of individuals heaving at one end will jockey the boat around enough so that the current's grip is broken.

PORTAGING

Most Canadian railroads will carry a canoe and stop anywhere to pick up or let off. This is an uncommon practice in the U. S. Across the North, the bush pilots will fly canoes and outfits in and out anywhere.

When it comes to portaging, discretion continues to be the wiser part of valor, particularly when one is more or less a greenhorn in this new canoeing world. Especially when a trail around rapids seems to be well traveled, it will be well to heed such eloquent counsel. On most canoe trips of any length, one or more portages will be necessary, perhaps a carry from one lake to another or an overland route around a stretch of white water. If it is not exceptionally windy and if you are traveling as light as you should be, then the work will not be too strenuous, even when you are alone. In fact, it often feels good to get out and stretch your legs.

Ideally, it will be possible to complete a portage in two carries. On the first trip over, take the packs. At this time, armed with an ax, it will be possible to scout out the trail and to clear away any obstructions. Finally, come through with the canoe itself.

Perhaps the carry will take place at tea time. If so, build the bright lone fire at the launching end. It is both a psychological and a physiological error to rest *before* a portage. For one thing, muscles stiffen. For another, the task looms all the more formidable. To boil the kettle is all the more gratifying when all that remains to be done, after making sure that every last spark is extinguished, is to board the portaged and repacked canoe and set forth once more.

If you are traveling with a map, depending of course on the remoteness of the region, portages may be charted. Otherwise, stop and look for them at the sound of white water. The portage trail, if any, will be along the line of easiest going. It may, of course, be on either side of the ford. The landing place is usually obvious, perhaps because of blazes, topped trees, clearings, dead Indian fires, or litter.

In crossing overland from one lake to another, look for a dip in the hills. The earliest individuals to use such a portage wanted to make it as easy as possible. In the old days, such portages were frequently marked by blazes or by the lopping off of the higher branches of a conspicously high tree, some of which may still stand.

SHOULDER PROTECTION

The most arduous portage begins with one step, and that will be more comfortable to take when some provision is made for padding between the canoe and the shoulders. This may be only the flats of the lashed paddles, plus extra folded shirts or such. The stern should again be slightly lower than the bow, making for better vision.

On short carries, the lightweights are sometimes carried upright and unpacked by two men, the keel resting on the shoulders. It then becomes all the more important for the

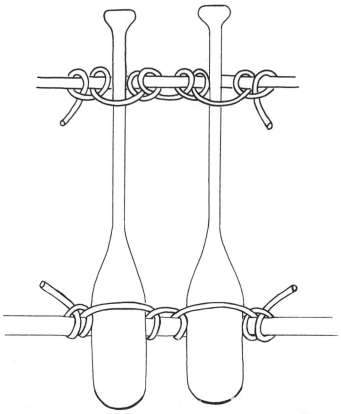

Portage Yoke Fashioned by Lashing Canoe Paddles to Thwarts

partners to maintain the same rhythm in walking, usually a process that requires considerable concentration because of the unevenness of the ground. A good waltzer has more luck in carrying a canoe, as a gliding walk rather than a bouncy stride helps keep the weight from continually jabbing into the neck and shoulders. Caution should be exercised on all carries so as to avoid falls and sprains.

Incidentally, bugs may be a bother when you are occupied in keeping the canoe balanced on your shoulders. During fly season, apply plenty of repellent, for few things are more distracting than mosquitoes whining in the enclosed stuffiness directly above your imprisoned head.

LIFTING

The secret to lifting lies in tossing instead of pressing. If alone, roll the emptied and unpacked upright canoe away from yourself on one side and take hold of the improvised yoke or the center thwart. With an upward jerk of the arms and a forward shove of the knees, toss the canoe up and around. Your knees will support the bulge of the canoe briefly when it is halfway up. Then when the canoe is tossed and bounced nearly upside down, duck your head into position in front of the yoke or center thwart. This way, your two hands and knees will get the canoe up without straining or even over-exerting your back and arms.

When two partners are involved, the lift is easy. Again the canoe is started right-side-up. The bowman stands slightly ahead of the front seat, the stern man a bit ahead of the rear seat. Each reaches down and grips the gunwales. Then, on

signal, you lift together, rolling the canoe over as it is hoisted. The seats can become the carrying yokes.

The greenhorn working by himself can, until he gains experience, instead prop the bow against a rock or tree, get into position under the thus half-raised canoe, and easily bring it in balance across his shoulders and neck. When one man will be carrying the canoe, the other the duffle, then the second canoeist can half-lift the craft for his partner.

With a carry longer than 50 yards, some sort of padding will make things a lot easier. Many canoeists just put on a down or flotation jacket.

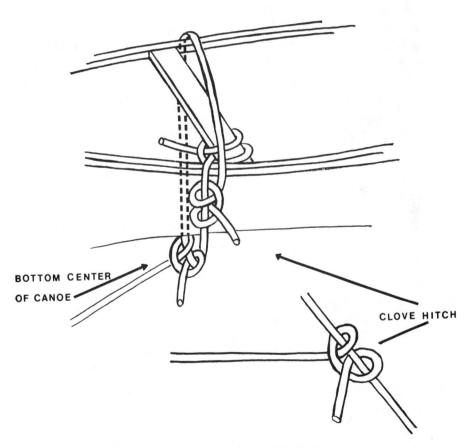

BOTTOM CENTER
OF CANOE

CLOVE HITCH

Rope Arrangement for Lining a Canoe

LINING THE CANOE

The major secret in lining the canoe is to get the front rope hauling the canoe just above the waterline. This can be accomplished most conveniently from a ring attached to the outer portion of the prow. Lacking this, run a rope around the boat, top and bottom, and tie the line to the under center of this. Both methods will cause the bow to lift slightly under pressure, as it should; this is also the correct method of tying on for towing. When, as is usually done instead, the line is attached to the gunwale, the bow dips and ploughs erratically.

When two men are lining a canoe, you'll also need a stern line, a good provision even with one man. Depending on the water, both of these ropes can be up to about 100 feet long. Then, walking or wading as best you can along the shore, one or two individuals can pull the floating, usually loaded craft through an otherwise unnavigable stretch of water. When the duffle is left in the canoe, incidentally, it should be centered low in the craft so that the canoe can spin easily at either end.

Using the current and the ropes, the canoeist can steer the craft to a certain extent. Pulling on the bow and easing the tension on the stern will cause the craft to move shoreward. The opposite of this, a tight stern and a loose bow, will urge the canoe outward into the current. Despite all this, and because of currents, both maneuvers become tricky at times, and either individual can also carry a pole with which to fend the canoe. Too, one partner can ride the canoe with a pole, although balance then often becomes a considerable problem.

Canoes are also lined downstream, whereupon most of the brawn is used in holding them back.

CHAPTER 10

Handling Your Own Pack Train

You're at the jumping-off place.

Maybe this is a fog-sodden wharf in Alaska. Perhaps it is somewhere along the Alaska Highway in British Columbia or the Yukon. Possibly it is where a dirt road halts against a mountain. Or the place may be a remote western airport almost anywhere. A loose-limbed fellow with a grin stretching his freckles begins ambling your way.

"I take it you're the hombres who've had me hitched to a ballpoint pen?" the outfitter asks. "Well, your horses are itching to hit the trail. What fishing gear did you finally bring?"

It's been your lifelong ambition to fish a camp in the horse country of the continental West. Here most of the really fine backwoods lie at least several days and usually farther from the closest steel or the nearest four-wheel drive or wagon road, and although planes are taking over to a certain extent these days, the cheapest and most common method of transport on any extended trip is with pack animals. These can be arranged for beforehand, for hire or even purchase. Well, by tomorrow, you'll finally be forking that saddle.

At the base camp where they are preparing for another trip, this one with guides, you shake hands with the wrangler. You swap the busy cook a hello for his grunt. You take a doubtful look at the salt-licking buckskin who's going to be both your transportation and your companion for the next few weeks.

Somewhere in the midst of a confab that builds between the outfitter and the wrangler about the best way to get within photographing distance of that grizzly they've glassed a few hours away, the sizzle of steaks begins asserting itself. The cook lets go with a heartfelt whoop. As you and the others turn toward the billowing cook tent, your saddle horse surprises you with a velvet-nosed nuzzle.

All of a sudden you realize that this trip that you and a companion have been planning for so long is really going to be something. You hope that you can pull your own weight. If only you knew a little bit more about what lies ahead. . . .

The outdoorsman who finally gets around to that long-awaited pack trip has almost invariably picked up plenty of wilderness savvy along the way. He's generally a top backwoodsman, to boot. The only things he hasn't had much chance to become familiar with beforehand are western horses and gear. The following observations may help to acquaint this otherwise experienced outdoorsman with what the pack animal journey holds for him.

PACK ANIMALS

A large pack mule will freight more than a horse unless it happens not to be in the mood. Pound for pound, so will a burro. But among the disadvantages to be met with both mules and burros is that it becomes nigh impossible to make many of them ford rivers and even fair-sized creeks, or to cover really boggy and muskegy country. The result is that their use is confined almost exclusively to desert and high, arid regions.

For general transportation, the more amenable horse is commonly used. How much one of these can pack day after day depends on a combination of details and approximations having to do with terrain, weather, type of load, gear, food, skill of the human packers, and the aptitude and temperament of the individual animal.

An average grass-fed horse, to generalize, can be expected to pack about 140 to 180 pounds for weeks at a time along the steep trails to be found in high country. Many times this minimum can be increased. To load an animal beyond its

usual limit for very long, however, makes for all kinds of trouble, including incapacitating sore backs. This limiting figure, whatever it may be, will suggest the number of pack animals called for to handle a particular outfit. There is this, too. Food supplies are apt to lessen as the pack train progresses, although you may also be picking up additional weight, as in the form of ore samples.

Along reasonably decent going, the usual pack horse or mule can average about 15 miles a day, starting about 10 A.M. and stopping about 4 P.M. Burros are much slower. The location of good graze and water is what ordinarily determines the picking of the camping areas and, therefore, the duration of the day's journey.

Plenty of water and graze exists throughout much of the western reaches. This is all to the good, for otherwise the animals, even though hobbled and belled, will stray for miles in search of nourishment. Where there there is ample fodder, it is reasonable even in the wilder regions to take a pack string through almost any area where steep cliffs, very heavy forest, and downfall do not bar the way. Almost all the western forests, except those on the thick southern sides of some mountains and the jackpots resulting from Indian or lightning-set fires and requiring that you ax your way, are open enough to ride through freely nearly everywhere. Even where you do not see an open trail, your animal will many times find one, particularly if it is in familiar country.

LEARNING TO RIDE

The prospective rider who has not previously journeyed with a pack string should understand certain details about the horse and his load, as well as some of the procedures of traveling and camping. These vary somewhat in different localities and among various outfits. Basically, however, they're hitched to the proposition that keeping the livestock in good condition is the primary essential. For the purposes of this book, we'll mainly consider the problems of one or two outdoorsmen who are fairly well experienced with the ways of the wilderness although not necessarily with livestock.

That's the way I started out, and because I suppose that my particular problems were rather characteristic, let us consider them. For one thing, except for riding farm animals on my Grandfather Adams's farm in western Massachusetts and later excursions on English saddles along Boston bridle paths, I knew nothing about riding. Nevertheless, once we had built our log cabin at Hudson Hope, British Columbia, my wife and I bought a couple of well-broken local cayuses, selected a flat open stretch downwind and downstream of our wilderness home, and put up a pole corral for them. I took the more unruly of the two for myself.

Riding the first few times as instructed by the horses' former owner made us stiff and sore, and there were areas where it removed skin, too.

"My knees feel it most," Vena said.

"So do mine, but they'll get toughened."

"I suppose it's the western saddles," my wife said. "I have to use my knees so much, along with my ankles, to take up the shock and to keep from bouncing."

"We'll get used to that," I said. "I'm not worried about that at all."

"There are places where I don't have any hide left," Vena said, "like the inside of both knees."

"It'll all work out," I said, "when we get the rhythm of it. That's it, I suppose, the rhythm."

"I don't know about Chinook," Vena said, "but Cloud has a lot of different rhythms, and when he isn't on a trail he adds a few more. It's not just a matter of keeping time the right way. I wish someone was around who could really teach us how to ride correctly."

"I don't think they know themselves what they do," I said. "They just grew up riding, and they never thought much of anything about it, just as we never thought about walking. We just tried, I suppose, and kept on trying until we were getting around."

"I suppose so, but that doesn't help much now."

"There may be a way," I told her. "King Gething told me that the best way to learn to ride naturally is to go on a trip for several days. By the time you're through, he said, you've learned in self-defense to stop irritating the sore spots you shouldn't have been making sore, anyway."

"Why don't we do it?"

"All right," I said. "Now that I've sent off that article on wild foods and the Chinaman Lake trip, let's accept King's invitation and ride up to his mine and back. It's not too rough cross-country, he said, and we'll come up against a lot of different kinds of terrain. Then we can get in some extra riding while we're staying there."

She didn't say anything for a moment. Then she smiled.

"When do we leave?" she asked.

"How about the day after tomorrow? There's something I want to do first."

"Where are you going now?"

"Riding," I said. "I'd like to go alone this one time if you don't mind. And would you keep the dog in, please?"

"You'll be all right?" she asked.

"If I can't handle Chinook when Cloud isn't along," I said, "it's time I was finding out."

Chinook was docile enough when I saddled her, although, as usual, she danced some when I was tightening the latigo and trying to get the bit past her teeth. She kept jerking her head toward Cloud while I was untying the halter shank, coiling it, and fastening it with a rawhide lace to the front of the saddle. Then, when I got the reins in my left hand, the saddle horn in my right, with my back to her head and my left foot awkwardly in the stirrup, she started before I was ready.

"Whoa," I was saying, "whoa!"

It was all right, though, because the forward impetus swung me into the seat. Then my off toe was groping for the iron stirrup which kept banging me on the ankle, and I was trying to turn her and to keep my balance, all at the same time. Cloud was whinnying. When Chinook crooked her head to answer, I managed to keep her head turned until she was going in the direction I wanted.

She had her mind made up that she was traveling to town and that, in any event, if she had to leave the grey gelding behind, she certainly wasn't going into the woods and upriver. By digging my heels into her ribs, I finally got her up past the cabin. Vena waved, and I heard her telling the Irish wolfhound to be quiet. Then we reached a loop of Bull Creek that Chinook decided she wasn't going to cross.

"How's about a drink," I said, as if we were both in this thing together and I wanted to be agreeable about everything. "Go ahead and have a drink."

I loosened the reins. She ducked her head several times, but the creek bed here was steep and narrow. She tried bending her front legs. She gave this up, though, when her bare hoofs slipped. Then she wanted to go back.

I turned her three or four times, bringing her again to the creek. She wouldn't cross it, although the water was no more than three feet wide, and the whole terrain was perfectly safe. When I went back down the trail a ways and then ran her for it, she reared at the last moment and stood there quivering.

There didn't seem to be any use in having a horse and not being able to manage her. The trouble, of course, was that I

wasn't sure of myself and that I didn't know anything about riding. Well, I decided, it was about time I learned what I could. Settling myself as solidly as possible, I reached up and broke off a poplar branch.

Just the motion set Chinook off, and she was across the brook in a single leap. The impetus shoved me hard against the stirrups, then slammed me into the cantle. I was thinking how she'd be reassured now that she'd found I'd been right and that there was nothing at all to the crossing. Then I was just thinking about how to stay on.

Chinook was running through the woods. Whenever an obstruction such as a log appeared in the way, she leaped it. Every few stops she bucked. If she had twisted at all, I would have been off after the first lunge or two. As it was, whenever I left the saddle, I always found it there to receive me again.

I was hammering against the leather so hard that my back ached. At first, I clung to Chinook with my thighs and knees while managing to keep enough spring in them and my ankles to take up some of the shock. I kept turning and ducking in an effort not to be swept off. Then I realized the strength was leaving my leg muscles. The pain knifing down from my hips to my shins didn't bother me too much because I didn't have time to think about it. But when all tension left my legs, leaving them limp, all I could do was grab for the saddle horn and hold on with all my might.

It was then that I learned something about balance. My body must have been equalizing itself automatically, for now that I was gripping the horn I was no longer an instinctively centering weight but, instead, a loosening sack attached to a peg. I tried to hold myself down in the saddle. Young poplars were flashing across me. A black stump loomed up in their midst. Chinook veered, and suddenly there was no longer anything beneath me but atmosphere.

I was yelling something. Then I was on my back in a patch of bunchberries. It wasn't any worse than being tackled hard in football, only I wondered why I wasn't just relaxing there instead of shouting and scrambling up. Then I realized I was yelling, "Whoa!"

Chinook was standing there, the two black reins trailing on the ground in front of her. She was breathing hard, and when she backed away from me and stepped on a rein, the resulting tug caused her to rear.

"Easy," I said, forcing my voice low and keeping my motions gradual. I didn't want her galloping back to the cabin riderless and frightening Vena. For that matter, maybe she wouldn't even stop at the cabin; saddled and bridled, she could get hung up somewhere. "Easy, now. Whoa."

Then my foot was on a rein. When she jerked back again, the tightening leather fairly straightened into my hand. I've wondered afterward why I tried again, alone out there in the woods. I suppose if I hadn't been alone, though, I wouldn't have had the temerity to risk making a spectacle of myself, although what I did seemed to be the only thing there was to do.

The second time was infinitely worse. My legs gave out sooner, not that the pain made much difference any more, but

I couldn't make them grip or take up any of the jar. I was bounced so high against the thumping saddle that it was difficult to maintain my seat.

I had very little control over my body any longer, and I had far less over Chinook. It wasn't that she was a bad horse in any sense, for she could have easily wiped me off by going under a low limb, while if she had put any twists in her straightforward bucking, I wouldn't have lasted a minute. It was more as if she'd been accustomed to being on her own and making her own decisions, and now she'd worked herself into such a state that she couldn't quit any more than I could.

She was running now through an old burn, and I could see the short, charred ends of poplar saplings like spears below me. That was when I grabbed leather again. The realization came to me, too, that she was pounding along the edge of the cliff which, with the way the Peace River kept undermining the shale, was treacherous at best.

I pulled on both reins, then sawed on them and eventually got her neck twisted so far that she began veering in a wide circle. That was something, at least, although her wildly plunging pace didn't slacken. When I tried to halt her by steering her into a great fallen spruce, fearful all the while of the crash that might result, she just disregarded the direction in which her head was being hauled.

What halted her finally, I don't know. I suppose the fact that I'd fortunately secured a stout bridle enabled me to tire out her neck muscles. She began turning in such a tight circle that she could no longer run, although when I thought I had her at enough of a standstill so I could descend safely, she gave a final pitch that sent me sprawling. This time, however, I kept hold of the reins.

My aching legs were trembling, but I noticed that she was quivering, too. Her heaving body was so white with sweat in places that, despite everything, I was sorry for her. But it was no time to think of that.

This time when I got into the saddle, I grasped the cheek of the bridle as firmly as I could and somehow found my right stirrup in a single, shaky motion. Than I tried to forget about

Chinook's mouth as I held her head as high as I could. She didn't seem to be able to get started running again, and each time she tried to pitch, I tugged her head higher.

Then, grimly, I turned her the way we'd come. She balked once more at the creek, and then she wanted to leap it, but partly because I was afraid I'd never survive another plunge, I made her walk across. Then I turned her and walked her back. I walked her back and forth through the water until she was doing it automatically.

Then, not relaxing the pressure of my left hand on the reins, I broke off another poplar branch. Scarcely daring not to leave well enough alone, I waved it back and forth by her head. Nothing happened. I brought it down easily against her flank the way I'd meant to that first time. Muscles twitched, but the only other effect was that she obediently picked up her pace. I took her back and forth across the stream again, and then, hot and exhausted, I headed her homeward.

Cloud whinnied as we approached, but Chinook gave no heed. She stood, head down, while I tied her halter rope, then pulled off bridle, saddle, and saddle blanket. She was so wet that on second thought, although I was sore and shaken enough not to feel much like it, I got an old piece of blanket and rubbed her until she was glossy. She just stood there, never moving while I worked all around her.

When I was finished, I stroked her gleaming neck. She turned her velvet nose and, to my surprise, softly nuzzled me.

"Did you have a good ride?" Vena asked when I went in.

"Yes, it was quite a ride."

She was looking at me with an intent expression, but I guess she could see I didn't want to talk about it, for she turned back to the stockings she was darning. She must have been worrying, I thought, because it usually took some sort of cataclysmic occurrence before she could get herself to do any darning.

"I had an idea that you might be back early," she said. "It looks so much like rain."

It wasn't that I made a practice of keeping anything from her. It was just that I didn't want her to worry. She didn't say any more about it, although just from the condition of my legs, which were raw in places and had stuck to my trousers, she could certainly tell that something had happened.

Then I realized that she'd concern herself needlessly if I kept silent, and that this worry would so spread to other things that she'd become afraid I might be concealing things from her if only for her own peace of mind. I told her then, and it didn't seem important any more.

"It might be just as well if you ride only Cloud for awhile," I said. "Not that I think I'm any better a rider than you, but I just don't want you getting hurt."

"I don't want you getting hurt, either," she said, "especially not alone out in the woods somewhere."

"I think Chinook and I understand each other now," I said. "I don't think she'll ever be any more trouble."

"I hope not," Vena said, putting down her work and coming toward me. "I think it's easy for me to understand Chinook a little bit, too."

DUTIES OF THE WRANGLER

You're already in the wilderness, say, with your partner and a saddle cayuse and two pack horses apiece. You're going to break camp and travel on this day. At the first quickening of dawn, the one whose turn it is to be wrangler starts out to find and drive in the animals which you turned loose the afternoon before to feed. All of them, probably, have hobbles strapping their front legs rather closely together. The bells buckled around the necks of the leaders and any recalcitrants will clang, bong, and peal the melody of their whereabouts.

Nevertheless, the horses may be feeding anywhere from a few yards to maybe a half mile from camp, although the experienced wrangler usually keeps an ear open. If before dark they start to drift too far, he'll often edge around and whoop them back. His own horse, if he can manage it, is staked nearby in a lush stand of grass at the end of a picket rope.

Trouble comes when the animals are not all out of the same bunch. Then they may be scattered in several groups. It can take a good half of the morning before both partners have located them all. Every once in a while delays of this kind must be expected. If a particular knothead becomes too much of a nuisance, though, it may be tied short to a tree all one night so it will keep so busy eating the next night that it won't have time to wander. When the wrangler drives the horses into camp, he ties them up by their respective saddles.

DUTIES OF THE COOK

In the meantime, the partner whose turn it is to be cook starts dishing out breakfast. Then he sees to it that both he and his sidekick get their lunches, in many cases put up the night before. After washing and drying the dishes, he packs the kitchen and the food panniers, making sure that what he needs for the next meal is where he can get at it. He then turns to with his partner to roll up the tent and finish getting the outfit ready to travel.

PANNIERS

There is no standard size for panniers. Most of them, the better ones, measure on the outside about 22 inches long, 15 inches high, and 9 inches wide from front to back. Packers in country where it matters prefer the bottom angled inward so the pannier will not stick out on the animal and bump into trees. A lower portion 6 inches wide will be functional.

The top, bottom, and sides can be made of ⅜- or ½-inch waterproof plywood, and the ends of ⅞-inch pine or spruce. To prevent mice and chipmunks from getting at the contents when they are vulnerable, the food panniers can be lined with metal or with copper screening. Notches on the front edges are made for the lash ropes that secure the pannier on the sawbuck saddle. Hinges and fasteners can be either metal or leather.

Various camp outfitters sell panniers, or kyacks as they are also called, made of fiberboard and plywood. If you cannot easily rent them, you also can build them yourself, as most bushmen do. Some are made of the heaviest canvas. Espe-

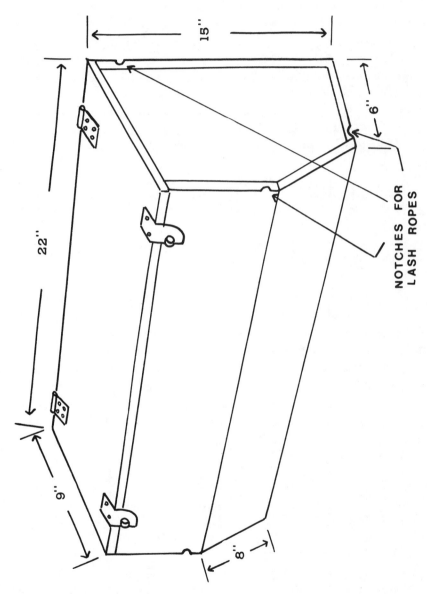

15"

6"

22"

9"

8"

NOTCHES FOR
LASH ROPES

Pannier

cially picturesque, although not as practical as the wooden variation, are those made of tough, untanned cowhide laced together with the hair outside.

SADDLEBAGS

Camera equipment is usually carried on the riding horse. So are binoculars. Saddlebags are handy for this purpose in open country. If you're sidling around among trees, though, anything fragile is better wrapped in your extra shirt or down jacket and tied securely behind the pommel.

Watch it, too, when you stop, for a lot of cayuses have a habit of occasionally rolling while still saddled.

Fishing rods can be a problem. Some stow them in or by stiff rifle scabbards slung from the side of the riding saddle. Often the best idea is to have a stout aluminum or fiber case for them and to trust them to the most reliable pack horse.

TARPAULIN

Sleeping bag and air or foam mattresses may be rolled in a tarpaulin about eight foot square, which later may serve as a ground cloth, and tied with a rope. Such a bundle will measure about three feet by a foot and a half. Often flat rather than round, it will be some seven or eight inches thick. It can, therefore, be conveniently laid atop the saddle and panniers. The pack cloth of heavy waterproofed canvas, spread over each packhorse load before the crosstree diamond, one-man diamond, squaw, or other hitch is thrown, will protect the equipment from moisture and from snagging in the brush.

Be sure that the ax in the sheath goes where it is both safe and readily accessible. On a pack horse, it generally can be shoved under the lashings with the handle angling backward and with the sheath strapped over a rope as an additional precaution against loss.

Ordinarily, you should place the most often used articles at the top of their particular panniers which, along with the pack

saddles, should be numbered to avoid confusion. Shirts and such can be used to wrap breakables. Tie possessions which dampness can ruin, such as camera equipment, securely within slightly inflated waterproofs. The oilskin variety was popular when I first took to the woods, but now lighter and far more secure plastic containers are cheaper and less bulky.

Equal weights must, as nearly as possible, be placed in each member of a pair of panniers so that the two will balance on the animal. It isn't a bad idea to carry a small bathroom scale for this purpose, as the panniers should be within two or three pounds of each other. Desirable maximum weights vary according to the animal. Fifty pounds is sometimes the limit.

Immediately after breakfast, then, each rider packs his own gear and bundles up his bedroll. He makes sure that he has on his person whatever he'll want during the day. He checks to see if his camera and extra clothing, including maybe a waterproof poncho, are ready to secure on his riding saddle.

PACKING LOADS ON HORSES

Two experienced individuals working together will pack a horse in about ten minutes when everything is at hand, and you soon become experienced. From this, you can figure approximately how long it takes you to get on the trail after the animals arrive. Every outdoorsman in horse country should learn how to pack. You never can tell when it may be necessary to lend a hand or to proceed on your own.

One mounts and dismounts from the left side of the horse as it faces forward. This is known, therefore, as the "on" or "near" side. Some horses become so accustomed to having this side the master side that they become skittish at any change.

When packing it saves time to work in pairs, but the offside person goes about the task as an assistant only, taking care of the tasks that can't be handled from the near side.

The first thing to make sure of is that the animal's back is clean. A curry comb and a brush will keep it well groomed and fit, especially if you are gentle with the animal at tender spots as where bones lie close to the surface. Care must be taken, too, that the saddle blanket is likewise as clean as possible. Never approach an animal, of course, before making it calmly aware of your presence.

SADDLE BLANKET

A good woolen saddle blanket, or other adequate pad, goes on initially. It must be smooth and soft. Throw it on close to the neck and then slide in toward the tail so that the hair will lie right. It should extend at least some three inches from where the saddle is to rest. When it has been smoothed into place, put a finger under its center front and back and lift it slightly from the backbone so as to provide ventilation, as well as to prevent the load from pressing unduly on the spine. The saddle goes on next.

SADDLING PACK HORSES

Some latigos (the long strap used to secure the cinch) have buckles. The trick with these is to make certain that all reasonable slack is taken up between the ring and the cinch, or the tongue of the buckle may slide loose and cause the load to slip.

More commonly, the off-side packer will hand you the cinch under the belly. Shove the latigo through the cinch and then continue it up through the ring on the saddle from the outside in. Depending on the length of the latigo and the size of the horse, repeat this until you have made at least two complete loops, one over the other. Although the saddle should be forward, the cinch must not be too close to the front legs, or friction will cause a sore. If the saddle has a rear cinch, do the same with that, only more loosely.

Now let the animal stand awhile, going on to saddle the others. A lot of horses, mules, and burros tense up at this stage and often take enormous breaths that will make for slack when they let the air exhale.

When you come back, shove your left hand between the animal and the cinch ring to keep the hide from wrinkling. Draw up on the latigo until it is so tight that you can barely get two fingers betweeen the leather and the animal. Secure with two half hitches to the saddle ring—in from the top on the left-hand side, out from the back, around to the front and across to the right, and down inside the loop made by the crossover. Tuck any remainder out of the way.

The rear cinch, which is fastened the same way, should go just behind the middle of the animal, but should not be as tight as the front cinch, lest it interfere with breathing.

SLINGING ON THE LOAD

Some panniers are made with leather loops or sling straps. When the panniers are smooth, a sling rope must be used to attach them to the pack saddle. This is an easy matter, however.

Take the light sling rope and, still standing on the near side, toss one end of it over the animal's back just ahead of the saddle. At about the middle of the rope, tie two half hitches or a clove hitch (see Chapter 9 for illustration of clove hitch) on the forward fork of the saddle.

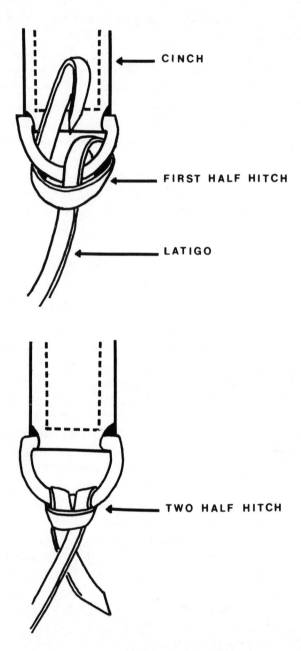

CINCH

FIRST HALF HITCH

LATIGO

TWO HALF HITCH

Cinching
Top: First step. *Bottom:* Second step.

Take the free end of the rope on your side and make a half hitch on the rear fork, leaving a large enough loop to go over the pannier. Bring the free end of the rope back and shove it under the loop. The same thing is done on the opposite side.

The off-side packer gets his pannier into place first because, with this routine, it is easier to remove this last when unpacking alone. Lift it well up into the forks. Hold it in position with the palm of the right hand. With the left hand adjust the loop around the lower side of the pannier. Pull up the slack with the free end of the rope where it passes across the middle of the pannier. Now tie a bowline in the end of the rope so this will reach the top center of the load. Flip the loop over the animal so it can be reached from the near side.

Now sling on the near pannier in exactly the same fashion, except that no bowline is tied. Instead, slip the end of the near rope through the bowline on the far side, draw everything tight, and tie off.

After the panniers have thus been slung and secured, lay what you choose across or between them and spread your pack cover into place. Then, with a strong half-inch rope braided to the ring of a canvas pack cinch which, at its other extremity has something such as a large wooden hook, bind down the entire load.

One of the hitches shown in the illustrations can be used for this purpose. This should be made as tight as possible, particularly as the tension will be on the pack and not on the animal. Get purchase when you have to by bracing a foot against the animal's side.

Bowline

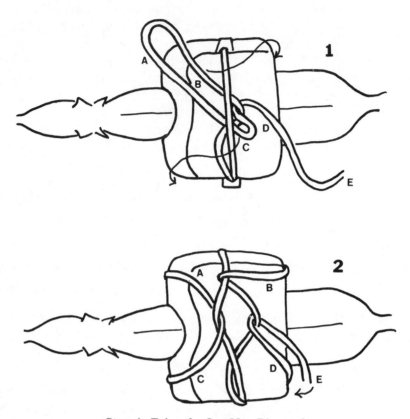

Steps in Tying the One-Man Diamond

Working from the on side of the animal, facing the tail, toss the cinch over the animal's back, reach under and pick up the cinch, and bind the running rope to the cinch hook from in to out. Pull up slack, run the loose rope up the side of the load, double, and then shove loop under the standing rope from back forward at the top of the pack to hold slack. Heave the running rope to the off side, go around there, and pull the free end of the running rope forward from the standing rope at the top of the load.

Put the end of the running rope over and under the forward end of the off load, then backward under the standing rope and pack, all as shown. Then pass the rope forward over the side of the load, double, and press the doubled part over and under the forward rope in a loop. Using the left hand, grab the double rope at loop just to the back of the standing rope. With the right hand pass the running rope down and close to the rear of the standing rope. Now pull up all slack.

Heave loose end across animal to the on side, across the center of the load. Move back to the on side and repeat what you've just done on the off side. Tighten everything. Finish off the hitch by passing the loose end of the line over and under the forward standing and running ropes, take up any slack with your foot braced against the load, and tie off.

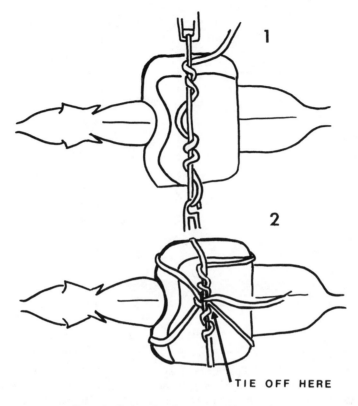

Steps in Tying the Crosstree Diamond

Stand at the on side of the horse, facing tail. Ease cinch over top of pack so that enough hangs loose under the horse's belly to be grasped and engaged in hook from in to out. Pull tight and hold by grasping the standing and running ropes in left hand.

Double loose part of running rope and thrust under standing rope from rear forward at top and middle of load. Then bring center of loop over and under standing rope again as shown, thus giving rope at either end of loop another complete turn around standing rope. Toss loose rope to off side of animal.

Go around back of the horse, with a reassuring hand on his rump, and bring line down along front, bottom, and back end of load, shoving rope end up through loop at top of pack. Take up slack and come back to on side of animal.

Pass running rope around front, bottom, and back end of what it is you're packing, then under the standing rope at the opposite middle of the loop. Take up slack, tighten all the way around, proceeding in sequence. Finish by pressing foot on load, pulling as tightly as you can, and finally tying off.

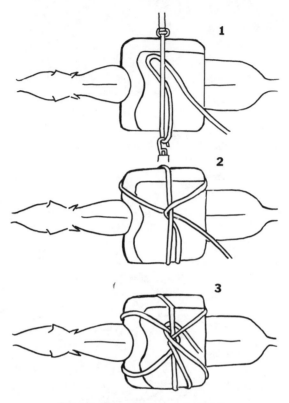

Steps in Tying the Squaw Hitch

Stand at on side of horse, facing tail. Toss the cinch over the top and middle of the pack so that you can readily reach it under the horse. Pass from in to out on the hook and draw up slack, being sure as always that the cinch passes smoothly under the middle of the horse's belly. Grab standing and running rope with left hand to keep tight.

With the right hand double the running rope, shoving this doubled part under the standing rope from rear forward in a bight as shown. Pull through sufficient slack line to make a loop big enough to pass over and around the off side of load. Move, carefully so as not to spook the animal, to the other side, turn loop over, and pass the loop around the ends and bottom of load from front to rear.

Come back to on side. There pass the running rope around the forward end, the bottom, and then the rear part of the load. Pull the end of the rope from above down, over, and beneath the standing, running, and back ropes at the top center of whatever it is you're packing. Starting at the beginning, tighten all the way around, bit by bit, pull taut, usually with the help of a foot braced against the load, and tie off.

Two packers can do a much faster job than one. The load must be smoothly installed and centered on all these hitches, then tightened evenly, or you're in for shifting packs and sore backs.

SADDLING TO RIDE

The natural tendency when saddling, especially with the heavier western rigs, is to heave the girth rings and stirrups too high. This causes them to bang noisily against such tender spots as leg points and ribs. A lot of resultant shying and sidestepping can be avoided by swinging these just high enough to land easily on your mount's back, where they'll slide down smoothly.

Or place the right stirrup and the cinch of the breeching across the seat of the saddle. Then, gripping the horn with the left hand and the back center of the saddle with the right hand, swing the saddle just high enough so you can settle it easily on the blanket. Incidentally, you'll probably get so that you'll be able to do this with just one hand on the horn. Go around and straighten up, at the same time taking down the stirrup, cinch, or breeching.

The same fundamentals that apply to readying the animal for the pack saddle apply when it comes to saddling for riding. The knees are not used in western riding as they are in the East. With the western saddle, therefore, the stirrups should be long enough so that you'll clear the seat by about two inches when standing in them. You'll then be able to rely on balance and on the grip of your thighs, employing your partly tensed knees and ankles as springs to absorb any roughness that would be jarring or jolting. There is a tremendous difference in horses in this respect. Without exaggeration, a very few actually trot more smoothly than others can walk.

MOUNTING AND RIDING

A smooth and sure way of getting into the western saddle is to take the lines in the left hand, stand to the left of the head of the animal and, facing the tail, secure a firm grip on the bridle cheek with the left hand, put the left foot lightly in the stirrup, grab the horn securely with the right hand, and then swing aboard in one fluid motion while using the horn as a pivot. This natural arc is spoiled, as we can readily understand, by the awkward, if common, habit of grasping the back of the saddle with the right hand.

In any event, when you're ready to get on, particularly if you and the animal are strangers, the main thing is to be in control. Horses differ. With a very few, you'll have to rein the head around, forcing the animal into a turn while it insists on moving ahead before you're ready. Others begin to fret and to pitch if you're heavy on the bit. Mostly, a firm but light hold on the lines will be sufficient.

Keep the lines low ordinarily, although if a knothead is inclined to pitch, you may want to curb that impulse by holding its head high. Don't fall into the practice, very common among dudes, of knotting the ends of the reins together as soon as you climb on a strange horse. Then, if anything goes wrong or even if you get off for some reason, you're apt to find yourself plumb afoot.

The times when you want to ride reinless, twist them a couple of times around the horn and perhaps top with a single half hitch. Then, if anything goes amuck, the lines will soon be dangling, to halt the animal if it's been broken to ground-rein or to impede it long enough for you to have a chance to ease around and catch it.

HITTING THE TRAIL

When the outfit is ready to hit the trail, the lead rope of all but the front pack animal is tied to the tail, pack, or to a rope loop fastened for that purpose around the rear fork of the pack saddle on the horse ahead. The knot used is one that can be instantly jerked free if something goes wrong. The wrangler holds the head of the foremost animal and rides off.

Or, with the pack horses turned loose, occasionally with a wire mask on each so that it won't stop to graze, the wrangler starts ahead, and the other partner closes in behind. Occasionally, a horse bolts or strays out of line, and the rear man urges him back. This he does slowly and quietly, so as not to excite the string.

Some days may be full of all kinds of trouble; spooked horses, turning packs, and snagged or bogged-down animals. Little distance then will be covered. On other days, you may
traverse as much as a rousing thirty miles. The thing is to try
to keep the pack train moving, all the time watching for slip-
ping loads that will necessitate repacking on the spot.

The wrangler is the man to say where the next camp shall
be made. He is responsible for the horses, and he must stop
where the feed is good, where there's water, and where he can
hold the animals reasonably close. Of course, with two individuals it's often an equal partnership.

MAKING CAMP

Everyone generally turns to when camp is reached, catch-
ing the animals and tying them well apart. Preferably the

lead ropes should be secured at least waist high and short enough so that the animals can't step over them or become entangled in nearby brush.

Knots are loosened and panniers eased to the ground in pairs, in such a way that their marks can be easily identified. Ropes are coiled and laid together in one place. Pack covers are folded and stacked or, if the weather is foul, spread protectively over the gear.

Saddles, which have probably been selected to fit certain animals and identified by names or numbers, are lined over a convenient log or upside down on the ground. Blankets are spread out, down side up, over their respective saddles to dry. If precipitation is falling or threatening, all these may be stacked in piles beneath the waterproof pack covers.

Finally, after perhaps some grooming, hobbles and bells should be strapped on and halters removed so that the animals will not accidentally get hung up by them. These halters, with their attached lead ropes, should be suspended in one place, away from little forest folk who would gnaw them for their salt.

PACK HORSE TRIPS FOR TWO

There is no reason why two individuals reasonably accustomed to handling horses, to camping in the wilderness, and to traveling safely in strange country should not take an extended pack horse trip by themselves. It means a lot of work for, if we fish for instance in virgin waters during the day, we will have cooking, tackle repairs, and odd jobs to take care of sometimes late into the night. Horse wrangling, too, will frequently interfere.

Two outdoorsmen can rent—or often more cheaply buy— four to six horses and live the life for months at a time. As for taking care of your own animals, lone trappers and prospectors often travel with six and seven.

Or, to a lesser extent, we can do the same thing with mules. In many ways most easily of all, one or both of us can pack gear on one or two burros and hike wherever we want to go.

THE TONIC OF WILDNESS

As Thoreau said, "We need the tonic of wildness—to wade sometimes in marshes where the bittern and the meadow hen lurk, and hear the booming of the snipe; to smell the whispering sedge where only some wilder and more solitary fowl builds her nest, and the mink crawls with its belly close to the ground.

"We can never have enough of nature. We must be refreshed by the sight of inexhaustible vigor, vast and titanic features, the wilderness with its living and its decaying trees, the thundercloud, the rain.

"If you have built castles in the air, your work need not be lost; that is where they should be. Now put the foundations under them."

INDEX

221